THE HISTORY OF THE CENTRAL INTELLIGENCE AGENCY (C.I.A.)

ANTONELLA COLONNA VILASI

authorHOUSE®

AuthorHouse™ UK Ltd.
1663 Liberty Drive
Bloomington, IN 47403 USA
www.authorhouse.co.uk
Phone: 0800.197.4150

Published by AuthorHouse 03/20/2014

ISBN: 978-1-4969-7553-9 (sc)
ISBN: 978-1-4969-7552-2 (hc)
ISBN: 978-1-4969-7554-6 (e)

CONTENTS

PREMISE

Cinema and literature have returned a romanticized image of the CIA as the spy agency whose agents were characterized by a great lack of scruples in means and methods to achieve their ends (until a license to kill) and a strong antagonism against their colleagues from other countries.

In fact, the role and purpose of this agency are clearly set out in its charter, which describes it as an agency under the United States intended to provide estimates functional to the maintenance of national security and the affirmation of the right of self-determination of States[1].

---

[1] "The CIA is an independent agency responsible for providing national security intelligence to senior US policymakers. The Director of the Central Intelligence Agency (D/CIA) is nominated by the president with the advice and consent of the Senate. The Director manages the operations, personnel, and budget of the Central Intelligence Agency" (www.cia.gov—accessed January 2014).

In pursuit of this goal, the charter of the CIA is based on solid ethical principles; however, over the decades, these have rarely been observed. The agency's mission, in fact, speaks to safeguard the United States[2] and highlights the moral requirements of its agents for service rendered to the nation[3], integrity[4], reliability[5], preparation[6], courage[7] and ability to work in group[8].

Relying on these qualities, the CIA agents are able to bring to fruition the tasks that the United States government

---

[2] "Preempt threats and further US national security objectives by collecting intelligence that matters, producing objective all-source analysis, conducting effective covert action as directed by the President, and safeguarding the secrets that help keep our Nation safe" (www.cia.gov—accessed January 2014).

[3] "Service. We put Nation first, Agency before unit, and mission before self. We take pride in being agile, responsive, and consequential" (www.cia.gov—accessed January 2014).

[4] "Integrity. We uphold the highest standards of lawful conduct. We are truthful and forthright, and we provide information and analysis without institutional or political bias. We maintain the Nation's trust through accountability and oversight" (www.cia.gov—accessed January 2014).

[5] "Stewardship. We preserve our ability to obtain secrets by protecting sources and methods from the moment we enter on duty until our last breath" (www.cia.gov—accessed January 2014).

[6] "Excellence. We bring the best of who we are to everything we do. We are self-aware, reflecting on our performance and learning from it. We strive to give our officers the tools, experiences, and leadership they need to excel" (www.cia.gov—accessed January 2014).

[7] "Courage. We accomplish difficult, high-stakes, often dangerous tasks. In executing mission, we carefully manage risk but we do not shy away from it. We value sacrifice and honor our fallen" (www.cia.gov—accessed January 2014).

[8] "Teamwork. We stand by and behind one another. Collaboration, both internal and external, underpins our best outcomes. Diversity and inclusion are mission imperatives" (www.cia.gov—accessed January 2014).

gives them, in order to address the challenges the country's government is facing in the context of international relations[9].

Due to these characteristics, the CIA has accompanied the entire history of the United States since the times of the Cold War and through all the critical moments of international equilibrium.

In this essay some of the most pivotal points in the history of the United States, trying to trace within them the status and the role of the CIA, are presented. History and politics texts have different interpretations of these moments, so it is not always easy to know the actual weight and the precise function of intelligence, especially in the case of the so-called "covert operations".

---

[9] "Key challenges: Close intelligence gaps with enhanced collection and analysis on the countries, non-state actors, and issues most critical to the President and senior national security team; Fulfill our global mission to give customers decision advantage as they confront an unprecedented volume and diversity of worldwide developments that affect US interests; Leverage technological advances for better performance in all mission areas—collection, analysis, covert action, and counterintelligence—while protecting against technological threats to the security of our information, operations, and officers; Improve the ways we attract, develop, and retain talent to maximize each CIA officer's potential to contribute to achieving mission; Better manage Agency resources during a period of fiscal austerity" (www.cia.gov—accessed January 2014).

Most likely, it will be the time to help the experts, but also public opinion, to formulate a more precise idea of these scenarios and give an account of an activity of intelligence that has lasted for decades and that, despite the criticisms and scandals, still occupies an important place in the United States political system.

CHAPTER 1

THE FOUNDATION OF THE NEW AGENCY

1.0. Introduction

The analytical component of the intelligence service's task is to transform the raw and purely quantitative information in actual "knowledge". This process is called "intelligence cycle" and is divided into five stages[10].

---

[10]   "The collection, analysis, and coordination of information useful to United states is the primary mission of the Central Intelligence Agency. At the heart of the mission lies the so-called intelligence cycle. The CIA defines the cycle as the process by which information is acquired, converted into intelligence, and made available to policymakers. The cycle has five phases: planning and direction, collection, processing, production and analysis, and dissemination [...], though, as a former CIA analyst notes, the 'cycle' is really less a series of discrete phases leading from one to another than a matrix of steady interaction between producers and consumers of intelligence, with multiple feedback loops" (Johnson L.K., America's Secret Power, New York, Oxford University Press, 1989, p. 76).

1. Planning and direction: the decision-making centers indicate the intelligence structures their interests and define the objectives of investigation and research[11];

2. Collection: aims to accumulate the maximum amount of information;

3. Processing: aims at processing information[12];

4. Production and analysis: tries to contextualize the information gathered[13];

---

[11]   "This step comprises the determination of intelligence requirements, preparation of a plan for collection, issuance of orders and requests to information-collection agencies. This step is also considered to be the beginning and the end of the cycle. It is the beginning because it involves drawing up specific collection requirements; it is the end because finished intelligence, which supports policy decisions generates new requirements" (Smith W.T., Encyclopedia of the Central Intelligence Agency, New York, Facts On File, 2003, p. 137).

[12]   "This step entails the acquisition of information and the provision of this information to processing or production elements. Information is collected from numerous OPEN SOURCE of intelligence (or OSINT), including newspapers, magazines, books, the Internet, and foreign television and radio broadcasts. Information is also collected from the various traditional intelligence disciplines, such as HUMINT (human intelligence), COMINT (communication intelligence), IMINT (imagery intelligence, formerly PHOTING for photographic intelligence), ELINT (electronic intelligence), MASINT (measurement and signature intelligence), TELING (telemetry intelligence), RADINT (intelligence gathered from radars), SIGINT (signals intelligence), and TECHNINT (technical intelligence)" (Smith W.T., Encyclopedia of the Central Intelligence Agency, cit., p. 137).

[13]   "In this step information is converted into finished intelligence through the integration, analysis, evaluation, and interpretation of all-source data and the reparation of intelligence products in support of known or anticipated consumer requirements" (Smith W.T., Encyclopedia of the Central Intelligence Agency, cit., p. 137).

5. Dissemination: the assessments and evaluations are distributed to decision-making bodies[14].

For the intelligence services the most difficult step is, of course, the fourth one as an error of assessment almost inevitably entails a bad choice from those who commissioned the analysis[15].

The decision-making centers, however, participate in the intelligence cycle in the planning and dissemination stage; this is the phase in which there is the greatest number of problems since the requests made to intelligence have not

---

[14] "In the final step in the cycle, finished intelligence is conveyed to consumers in a suitable form. Each day, finished intelligence is hand-delivered to the president and his key national security advisers. Certain policy makers receive finished intelligence. They may make on the basis of information decisions that lead to the need for more information. Thus the intelligence cycle continues" (Smith W.T., Encyclopedia of the Central Intelligence Agency, cit., p. 137).

[15] "§ 1905.4. Procedure for production. [...] (b) The General Counsel of CIA and Deputy Directors or Head of Independent Offices with responsibility for the information sought in the demand, or their designees, shall determine whether any information of materials may properly be produced in response to the demand, except the office of General Counsel may assert any and all legal defenses and objections to the demand available to CIA prior to the start of any search for information responsive to the demand. CIA may, in its sole discretion, decline to begin any search for information responsive to the demand until a final and non-appealable disposition of any such defenses and objections raised by CIA has been made by the entity or person that issued the demand" (National Defence, ed., LSA List of CFR, 32, Washington, U.S. Government Printing Office, part 800 to End, revised as of July 1, 2003, p. 435).

always represented the real needs or priorities[16]. On the other hand, the information receivers were not always fully satisfied from it[17].

1.1. **Previous events**

The United States was rather slow to adopt a structure of autonomous intelligence and independent from military forces (Army, Navy and Air Force) or from the departments in which was divided the United States executive. This slowness was due both to the institutional weakness of the government, and to the limited participation in the international events for most of the nineteenth century.

---

[16] One of the main problems concerning dissemination was to "establish uniform criteria for the determination of relative priorities for the transmission of critical national foreign intelligence, and advise the Secretary of Defense concerning the communication requirements of the Intelligence Community for the transmission of such intelligence" (US Central Intelligence Agency - CIA - Handbook. Strategic information, activities and regulations, Washington, International Business Publications, 2013, p. 262).

[17] For instance, in the course of the war in Iraq, "the United States was able to do a much better job of integrating the national intelligence effort by CIA, NSA, NRO and NIMA into the war-fighting effort, but coordination problems still remained, and war fighters note that overclassification, compartimentation, and restrictions on the release and dissemination of intelligence continued to present major problems. To put it bluntly, many actual users of intelligence in combat still see overclassification and disseminations as major problems and the security officers as much of a threat as the enemy" (Cordesman A.H., The Iraq War: Strategy, Tactics, and Military Lessons, Washington, Center for Strategic and International Studies, 2003, p. 185).

The United State Secret Service have always been characterized by a certain weakness. The inconsistency of the intelligence apparatus was due to the weakness of the executive and the strong distrust of large sections of the population towards structures that were secret and without public supervision. In addition, the isolation of the United States and their lack of involvement in international affairs and in the European conflicts of the nineteenth century is the second reason for the American delay in the field of intelligence. One of the main reasons which led the national states to build up their own structures for espionage and information gathering was the need to better understand the opposing powers, their industrial and military capacity, their secrets and their weaknesses[18].

---

[18]   "The way in which this coordination and synthesis should be accomplished had been a particular concern of the government, especially in this country. The necessity had been fully recognized by 1939. Representatives from the Department of Agriculture, Commerce, and the Interior were assigned to the Foreign Service as attaché. Their reports were made through the State Department. The military and naval attaché in American embassies and legations were less subject to coordination as their reports were directly to their respective services [...]. Woven with it is the issue yet to be fully settled. Should there be individual responsibility for estimating the intelligence which is sent to the policymaker, or should the representatives of the several interests involved take collective responsibility for that estimate?" (Darling A.B., The Central Intelligence Agency. An Instrument of Government to 1950, The Pennsylvania State University Press, 1990, p. 5).

A strong impulse was given to intelligence by the war, which resulted in the need to have information about the enemy, the more difficult to obtain during a conflict.

It was not until the Eighties of the nineteenth century that the Army and the Navy of the United States created its own information structures[19]. The Navy's one took the name of Office of Naval Intelligence (ONI) and was able to adopt the most advanced technology of the time. But in 1898 the war against Spain showed all the shortcomings of United States intelligence[20].

The early years of the twentieth century recorded a rapid progress in the field of technical and cryptographic security,

---

[19] "From the beginning, attempts to create a central intelligence organization ran into opposition from the State, war and Navy Departments. The State Department had traditionally been the source of foreign information, and the Army and Navy maintained their own intelligence operations, which they did not want to give up" (Darling A.B., The Central Intelligence Agency. An Instrument of Government to 1950, cit., p. 1).

[20] "During the years 1894-1897 the Naval War College and the Office of Naval Intelligence jointly prepared a series of contingency plans in the event of war with Spain. After the declaration of war on 22 April 1898, these plans were implemented with the U.S. North Atlantic Squadron attempting a blockade of Cuba [...]. Another intelligence target was the Spanish army in Cuba; the Office of Naval Intelligence pursued information about the Cuban countryside, Spanish movements there, and coordination with Cuba insurgents". The Office of Naval Intelligence did well in its first mission, that of providing timely intelligence on Cámara's squadron" (Dyal D.H., Historical Dictionary of the Spanish American War, Westport, Greenwood Press, 1996, p. 169)

and the United States found itself once again late not only with regards to Great Britain, but also to the other powers[21].

During World War I, indeed, all the major powers had strengthened their information equipment. Among these stood out that of Great Britain, where the Royal Navy had established a special structure (the famous Room 40), whose task was to intercept enemy codes. In 1916, Room 40 was able to decrypt the three major German codes[22].

In addition to the decryption, during the war there was a great recourse to Photographic Intelligence (PHOTINT) but,

---

[21] "Through history, cryptography has been used mainly to secure communications belonging to the powerful and the influential, usually governments, the military, and royalty [...]. In 1917 William Frederick Friedman, later to be honored as the father of U.S. cryptanalysis (and the man who conied that term), was employed as a civilian cryptanalyst [...] at Riverbank Laboratories and performed cryptanalysis for the U.S. Government, which had no cryptanalytic expertise of its own. Friedman went on to start a school for military cryptanalysts at Riverbank - later taking that work to Washington and leaving Riverbank" (Hansche S., Berti J-. Hare C., Official (ISC)2 Guide to the CISSP Exam, Boca Raton, Auerbach Publications, 2004, pp. 383-384).

[22] "In October 1914 [Sir William Reginald] Hall was appointed director of Naval Intelligence (DNA)- While at DNI, Hall oversaw Room 40 in the Old Admiralty Building of London, an intelligence office that monitored German diplomatic and military radio communications. Hall's Room 40 monitored and deciphered intercepted German radio signals, in part using the codebook captured from the German light cruiser Magdeburg. In May and June 1916, Room 40 intercepted radio signals that resulted in the Battle of Jutland. Room 40 also helped in the surveillance of Irish spies, such as Sir Roger Casement, and relayed other intelligence. One of the greatest accomplishments by Room 40 was the interception and decoding of the so-called Zimmermann Telegram on 17 January 1917" (Bandy J., Roberts P., Hall, Sir William Reginald, in Tucker S., ed., World War: A Student Encyclopedia, Santa Barbara, ABC-Clio, 2006, pp. 857-858).

despite technological progress, the main tool for gathering information was always the Human one (HUMINT)[23].

The war took on the characteristics of a fight in the trenches, while covert operations and paramilitary sabotage (the so-called "covert operations"), usually under the responsibility of the Secret Service, did not play a significant role. Instead, it was crucial to have information on the movements of enemy troops. In this field, Britain was able to build a real network of informants over the front able to provide information about the traffic of army trains[24].

Once at war, the United States was forced to rely almost entirely on British intelligence and managed to ensure an

---

[23]   Finnegan J.P., The Military Intelligence Story. A Photo Istory, Washington, U.S. Government Printing Office, 1998, p. 11.

[24]   "British strategic intelligence efforts, prior to the outbreak of war and during its early months [...] improved quickly. From 1916 to the end of the war, the Western Allies had good information about the German army from prisoner-of-war interrogations and analyses of captured documents" (Spencer C.T., The European Powers in the First World War: An Encyclopedia, New York, Routledge, 2013, p. 362).

adequate informational support to the American Expeditionary Force sent to fight in Europe[25].

This is because the action of the United States intelligence focused mainly on internal affairs. The responsibility of subversion and counter-intelligence was delegated largely to the War Department, which also used patriotic organizations such as the American Protection League[26]. The participation of private bodies to subversive activity and counter-intelligence was intense, although these were gradually replaced by the Federal Government.

In the period between the two wars, the intelligence apparatus of the Army and Navy underwent a radical dismantling. Within the Department of State a special office

---

[25]   "In the late 1930s [the British] worked to bolster American intelligence, first so that the United States would step up counterintelligence against Nazi efforts to undermine British supply lines from the western hemisphere, and later so that the United States would create a full-service intelligence system to supplement British efforts. As they judged correctly, this was in their immediate as well as as their long-term interest [...]. It was as a result of his interaction with the British that Donovan recommended creation of the first centralized U.S. intelligence organization, the Coordinator of Information (1941), and later of the OSS (1942)" (Godson R., Dirty tricks or Trump Card: U.S. Covert Action and Counterintelligence, New Brunswick, Transaction Publishers, 2001, p. 178).

[26]   "The history of 20th century dissent management is rife with popular spies. During World War I, the American Protective League (a volunteer citizen wing of the FBI predecessor Bureau of Investigation) provided information that led to detention of 50,000 citizens during the 'slacker raids'. Persuasion agents and opinion-leaders were deployed among the populance to stir up pro-war sentiments during WW1" (Bratich J.Z., Spies like us, in Packer J., ed., Secret Agents: Popular Icons Beyond James Bond, New York, Peter Lang Publishing, 2009, p. 134).

called U1, responsible for coordination and supervision of intelligence activities carried out by various agencies of the federal government, was created. Although this office was resolved very soon (1927), at its inside two of the principles considered to be of great importance in the future CIA were proclaimed: centralized control of intelligence and dominance of civilian authority over the military in operations management[27].

At the outbreak of World War II, the American intelligence system was still inadequate, so much so that the defeat at Pearl Harbor was declared the "intelligence failure". From then on, all the reforms of the United States intelligence services moved toward the prevention of a new surprise attack on the United States territory[28].

In June 1942 in the United States was established the Office of Strategic Services (OSS). At the head of this organization was William J. Donovan, a hero of the First World War and a Republican, close to the government of Churchill. Under Donovan's leadership, the OSS had responsibility for

---

[27]   "During World War I, U.S. intelligence efforts were limited to supporting the new American foreign policy doctrine of 'open diplomacy', reflecting the openess that permeated the thinking of U.S. policy makers at the time. To promote this new way of doing things, the State Department assumed the responsibility of coordinating all intelligence information, an effort that lasted until 1927" (Turner M.A., Why Secret Intelligence Fails, Dulles, Potomac Books, 2005, p. 19).

[28]   See Barrett K., Truth Jihad: My Epic Struggle against the 9/11 Big Lie, Joshua Tree, Progressive Press, 2007, pp. 165-166.

both analytical (screening and analysis of information), and operational (two military directives ascribed it, for example, the task of promoting propaganda, psychological warfare and covert operations) operations[29].

After World War II, the OSS was to coordinate the various systems of information available to the United States government and the director was supposed to be a civilian who had to answer directly to the President, without being subject to the chiefs of staff or to the departments of State. In this way it would have to cover a position equivalent to that of a military body[30].

But Harry Truman, who became president of the United States in 1945 following the death of Roosevelt, showed to be suspicious of OSS and decided to dissolve it in September of the same year, as soon as the war with Japan was over.

---

[29]   "President Roosevelt settled the issue by signing Executive Order 9128 on June 13, 1942; this removed FIS from COI and placed it under the new Office of War Information. What was left of COI became the Office of Strategic Services under the jurisdiction of the JCS. The JCS gave the OSS equal status with the other military services and authorized it to gather intelligence and conduct subversive activities and psychological welfare" (Liptak E., Office of Strategic Services 1942-1945. The World War II. Origin of the CIA, Oxford, Osprey Publishing, 2013, p. 5).

[30]   "Its role was to conduct overt and covert intelligence procurement activities in the war against the Axis Powers, including clandestine operations in support of planned military operations, to analyse 'raw' intelligence and disseminate finished intelligence reports to appropriate government agencies " (Stone D., Holocaust Testimony and the Challenge of the Philosophy of History, in Fine R., Turner Ch., eds, Social Theory After the Holocaust, Liverpool University Press, 2000, p. 214).

The termination of the OSS was part of the general process of the dismantling of the warfare system, but reopened the clash between the various departments and agencies of the United States government active in the context of intelligence. In this way, the United States found themselves devoid of an intelligence agency until 1946, when the creation of the Central Intelligence Agency (CIA) took place[31].

1.2. The foundation of the CIA

In January 1946, a new presidential directive established the Central Intelligence Group (CIG), who inherited most of the functions assigned to the OSS and was placed under the control of National Intelligence Authority (NIA), composed

---

[31]   "The abrupt end of OSS disguised a fundamental fact. President Truman, while not known to have devoted notable personal attention to issues of foreign intelligence before the fall of 1945, was already on the path of acting to establish a peacetime national foreign intelligence organization. In discussion with his budget director during the same month he signed the directive abolishing OSS, Truman indicated that J. Edgar Hoover's Federal Bureau of Investigation (FBI) should be cut back to prewar levels and confined to operations in the United States" (Garthoff D.F., Directors of Central Intelligence as Leaders of the U.S. Intelligence Community, 1946-2005, Washington, Potomac Books, 2007, p. 11).

of the Secretaries of State, the War, the Navy and a special representative of the Presidency[32].

The decree establishing the CIG did not put clear limits to its functions and its responsibilities. Just as with the case of the OSS, the failure to define the limits within which the CIG should have worked led to a strong antagonism between the new Central Intelligence Agency and the military intelligence services and the Department of State. The latter, actually, claimed its sole responsibility as to inform the President on the international situation and the foreign policy of the United States[33].

Broadening the perspective to the international context, the bipolar antagonism with the Soviet Union heightened the need for promoting the rapid consolidation of the institutional structure of American intelligence. For this reason, the creation of the CIA fell into this more general framework of

---

[32]   "[...] President Truman on 22 January 1946 created the Central Intelligence Group (CIG) - the direct predecessor of the CIA. Truman had realized the need for a centralized body to gather and coordinate intelligence information and to eliminate friction among competing military intelligence services. By the spring of 1946, the War Department's Strategic Services Unit was transferred to CIG, giving it the remnants of an OSS clandestine collection capability [...]. By June 1946, CIG had a strength of approximately 1,800 of which about one-third were overseas" (Paddock A.H. jr, U.S. Army Special Warfare. Its Origins. Psychological and Unconventional Warfare, 1941-1952, Honolulu, University Press of the Pacific, 2002, p. 40).

[33]   See Davis P.H.J., Intelligence and Government in Britain and the United States, Santa Barbara, ABC-Clio, 2012, p. 50.

reform of the security apparatus of the United States, which led to the birth of the National Security State[34].

The idea of Central Intelligence Agency raised many concerns in the political world and American public opinion, even within the same State Department and the White House itself. In particular, the fear of a possible military dominance in the future structure of intelligence that would have further supported the process of "militarization" of the United States foreign policy raised again.

However, despite these concerns, in 1947 the government decided to submit through Congress the bill on the reform of the security system, which also included the establishment of the Central Intelligence Agency (CIA). The parliamentary debate focused on the major concern of the White House: the possibility that the future Director of Central Intelligence (DCI) could be a soldier, as was the case for the CIG. At the end of the discussion, it was agreed that a soldier would be appointed as Director, but it was also specified that in that case he would have no obligation to the membership body,

---

[34]   See Raskin M.G., The Politics of National Security, New Brunswick, Transaction, 1979.

would not be subjected to any control by the latter and would be joined by a Deputy civil[35].

Approved by the Congress and ratified by Truman in the summer of 1947, the National Security Act stipulated that the CIA worked autonomously from the departments (from which the CIG depended on budget and men), and were subjected to the supervision and control of the Board of national security. The CIA Director should have been appointed directly by the President of the Council and approved by the Senate[36].

The main task assigned to CIA was to provide advice and guidance to the National Security Council, directing and coordinating the activities of the various intelligence structures of the United States government and providing

---

[35] "The Central Intelligence Agency was created by the National Security Act of 1947 [...]. The intelligence function is admittedly difficult, particularly for a democracy. By its very nature, the gathering, processing, and dissemination of intelligence must be to some degree secret, yet democracy as a system of governance is based on public accountability that requires transparency. There is, then, a tension, or even paradox, inherent to intelligence operations under democratic scrutiny, that is experienced in even - perhaps especially - the oldest, most well-established democracies, were citizens are accustomed to asserting their constitutional rights" (Bruneau T., Patriots for Profits: Contractors and the Military in U.S. National Security, Stanford University Press, 2011, p. 88).

[36] "The scope and ambition of the 1947 National Security Act was astonishing. It created a National Military Establishment, which became the Department of Defense in 1949. It gave the Air Force an independent status and provided the Joint Chiefs of Staff with statutory identity. It established the National Security Council (NSC), the Central Intelligence Agency (CIA), and a cluster of lesser-known institutions, including the National Resources Board, the Munition Board, and the Research and Development board" (Stuart D.T., Creating the National Security State: A History of the Law that Transformed America, Princeton University Press, 2008, p. 8).

for the assessment, development and distribution of the evaluation and analyzes produced. The National Security Act finally assigned to the CIA those tasks and those functions relating to intelligence that the National Security Council had "from time to time identified". This step was deliberately vague and generic, in order to allow the CIA to undertake a series of covert operations for which, according to the text of the law, lacked any authorization[37].

The birth of the CIA represented a turning point for the United States intelligence. The differences between the CIA and the CIG were not only formal; for the first time in American history the establishment of a central agency intelligence was legitimized by the vote of the Congress. The status and importance of the CIA were now higher than those of the two bodies that had preceded it (OSS and CIG),

---

[37] "The Central Intelligence Agency (CIA) was created by the 1947 National Security Act. It assigned the CIA the following tasks: (1) to advise the National Security Council (NSC) on intelligence matters related to national security; (2) to make recommendations to the NSC for the coordination of departmental and agency intelligence activities; (3) to correlate, evaluate, and disseminate intelligence; (4) to perform for the benefit of existing intelligence agencies such additional services as the NSC determines, and (5) to perfomr 'other functions and duties' relating to national security intelligence as the NSC may direct. Absent in this listing of tasks is any explicit authorization to engage in covert action or to collect its own information. Both of these tasks, however, quickly became part of its organizational mission" (Hastedt G.P., Encyclopedia of American Foreign Policy, New York, Facts On File, 2004, p. 67).

although it continued to be in a dependent position towards the main subject of American foreign policy[38].

1.3. The golden age: the Cold War

The belief that the Soviet Union was a totalitarian and expansionist power, ready to resort to any means to achieve their goals, legitimized the covert operations as necessary instruments of American foreign policy. Such use was supported by some of the representatives of the Truman administration, such as diplomat George Kennan, then head of the Policy Planning Staff of the State Department, who in 1948 encourage to "fight fire with fire" and also make use of unorthodox instruments in order to curb the threat posed by Communism. Two years later, a famous framework document (NSC 68) of American foreign policy drawn up by

---

[38]   See Smith W.T., Encyclopedia of the Central Intelligence Agency, cit., p. 6.

the National Security Council, was issued in coherence with this politics[39].

The early years of the Cold War were therefore characterized by the belief, from the Truman administration's side, that clandestine operations against the Russian and the European communist parties, especially the Italian and French ones, had to be promoted.

Between 1947 and 1948 two directives of the National Security Council appointed CIA with the responsibility of covert operations through the creation, at its inside, of a special structure called the Office of Policy Coordination (OPC)[40].

The first significant covert operation was the American intervention in Italy in the months preceding the elections in April 1948. Much of the operation was clear: the United States intervened in the election campaign by making positive

---

[39]   "Once the National Security Council approved NSC 10/2 Kennan actively participated in its implementation and ensured that his prerogatives as State Department representative were guaranteed. In discussion with Hillenkoetter and Souer in August 1948, Kennan stated that he would need to have specific knowledge of the objectives of every operation and also the procedures and methods employed in all cases where those procedures and methods involved political decisions. Kennen claimed the responsibility to decide which individual projects were politically desirable. The political warfare activity would be conducted as an instrument of U.S. foreign policy" (Miscamble W.D., George F. Kennan and the Making of American Foreign Policy, 1947-1950, Princeton University Press, 1992, p. 109).

[40]   See Turner M.A., Historical Dictionary of United States Intelligence, Lanham, Scarecrow Press, 2006, p. XXVIII.

propaganda for themselves and their allied Italian political forces. The clandestine dimension of the operation, however, was the financing of major non-communist parties, such as the Christian Democrats, the Republican Party and the Socialist Party of Italian workers. Being it a form of interference in the internal affairs of another country, the funding was made with "not documented funds" that were passed to the Italian political forces through the CIA.

The hidden aid of the United State was not decisive for the outcome of the election (in which the Socialists and the Communists were defeated while the Christian Democrats came out as the definite winners), but it was very important from a symbolic point of view. In the government of the United States, actually, emerged the belief that the means by which to defeat communism had been identified in the covert operations. The Italian affair became a model for the United States diplomacy, whose universal applicability was based on three fundamental elements: the presence of local pro-American actors to train and get to work, the availability of clandestine funds to be allocated to such people and the existence of a headquarter that would coordinate the operation and allocated the funding. This task was assigned to the CIA[41].

The United States covert operations in Europe addressed also the field of trade unions. Since 1948 the CIA cooperated with the leading American union (the American Federation of Labor—AFL) in providing support to non-communist trade unions in Italy and France. This covert operation was financed using a portion of the percentage of funds under the Marshall Plan (5 %) addressed to the Member States to cover administrative costs.

The United States objective was to facilitate the creation of trade unions and corporate contractarians, more receptive to the United States' reformist projects than were the trade unions, put under the hegemony of the Communists and Socialists. However, the Unite States plans actually clashed with a reality much different from what it was expected. In Italy, for example, there wasn't and never was going to be any large unified anti-communist trade union because the CISL, led by the Democrat Giulio Pastore, was a Catholic

---

[41]   "The Christian Democratic victory in Italy soothed some of Kennan's anxieties concerning the Soviet threat to the Mediterranean. It also provoked further consideration on his part of the most appropriate measure to turn back the Soviet challenge. The covert activities of the CIA impressed him and in May 1948 he recommended the creation of a permanent organization capable of undertaking the kind of mission that the CIA had performed in Italy on a rather ad hoc basis" Miscamble W.D., George F. Kennan and the Making of American Foreign Policy, 1947-1950, cit., p. 106).

organization, and the more reformist members of non-communist trade unionism gave life to their own organization (the future UIL)[42].

A third type of covert operation activated by the CIA was that carried out in the Soviet Union and the countries of the Communist bloc. It consisted of the anti-Communist propaganda, promoted through two radio stations, especially created and financed by the CIA (Radio Liberty and Radio Free Europe). Alongside this activity, there was also an attempt to infiltrate agents into so-called denied areas. The project was carried out in collaboration with the British Intelligence Service (MI6) and the organization of Reihnard Gehlen (former director of information for the East of the Nazi army), who then worked with the Western powers. The areas selected for this operation were initially Lithuania and Ukraine, where the presence of anti-Soviet partisan movements was stronger. The beneficiaries were mainly recruited among the Lithuanian and Ukrainian emigrants who were in the western parts of Germany, what a few months later would become the Federal

---

[42]   "Since the Soviets utilized the Communist parties to penetrate and dominate trade unions, liberal magazines, and other influential targets in the West, [Kennan] proposed that the United States use its far larger resources to penetrate and control these same institutions, for its national interests, while also applying pressure on the Soviet hierarchy through a sustained series of clandestine operations aimed at destabilizing the Soviet bloc countries" (Chester E.T., Covert Network: Progressive, the International Rescue Committee, and the CIA, Sharpe, New York, 1995, p. 25).

Republic of Germany. Trained by Gehlen's organization, these agents were parachuted in Ukraine and Lithuania. Once at their destination, they would have to make contact with the locals, but they were almost always discovered by Soviet counterintelligence, which could rely on information provided by spies inside the Western services[43].

The most ambitious and most expensive covert operation sponsored by the CIA and MI6 in the immediate post-war period, the operation *Valuable* in Albania, had a similar outcome. Scheduled at the end of 1948 and carried out between 1949 and 1951, it was a kind of paramilitary action such as those organized in Ukraine and Lithuania. The project devised by the CIA and MI6 involved the infiltration of small armed groups in the territory of Albania. Coordinated and directed from the outside, they would have to carry out acts of terrorism and military actions through which destabilize the country and overthrow the communist leader Enver Hoxha. In the United States and Great Britain's intention, the operation was also supposed of testing the effectiveness of covert paramilitary operations. The choice of Albania as a theatre of this experiment was dictated mainly by geographical

---

[43]   "General Reinhard Gehken had been the head of the German army's intelligence service for the Eastern Front. With the Nazi regime crumbling, Gehlen had hidden his files relating to Soviet military targets, and then waited for the final collapse" (Chester E.T., Covert Network: Progressive, the International Rescue Committee, and the CIA, cit., p. 85).

reasons: Great Britain, actually, had its own bases in the Mediterranean, and Albania was not territorially contiguous with the rest of the Communist bloc, and was bordered by two states hostile to Russia: Yugoslavia and Greece[44].

As the previous actions, the *Valuable* operation ended in a dismal failure as well. The few infiltrated survivors told that Hoxha's secret service knew Anglo-American plans and were ahead, waiting for the agents who came down in a parachute or arrived by sea. Many have suspected that within the Western intelligence services there was a soviet informant that would report to Russia[45].

The failure of these early covert operations caused the deterioration of relations between the British and United

---

[44]   For a general survey on the Operation Valuable in Albania see Trahair R.C.S., Encyclopedia of Cold War Espionage, Spies, and Secret Operations, Enigma Books, New York, 2013; Jeffery K., MI6: The History of the Secret Intelligence Service 1909-1949, London, Crowd, 2010; Dorril S., MI6: Inside the Covert World of Her Majesty's Secret Intelligence Service, New York, Touchstone, 2002.

[45]   It is believed that this character was Kim Philby, recently appointed liaison officer between MI6 and the CIA in Washington and one of the two British members of the United States - Great Britain Committee, responsible for covert operations in Albania (see Kilby K., My Silent War: the Autobiography of a Spy, London, Arrow Books, 2003).

States intelligence services and a drastic reduction of their collaboration[46].

On the domestic front, however, the enthusiasm for covert operations did not drop immediately, and CIA identified immediately new areas toward which direct their activities. This enthusiasm had originated from the Cold War mentality, but also from the growing frustration over the liabilities of the United States foreign policy, which in those years tended towards the "containment" of the Soviet Union. The increasing legitimacy of the CIA corresponded so to a constant expansion in terms of manpower and material resources of the structure of the CIA in charge of covert operations, i.e. the OPC[47].

---

[46]   "In 1950 they pulled out of Operation Valuable. Cooperation between the two sides had never been forthcoming. Apparently, Anglo-American frictions plagued the operations at all levels. Not only did they fail to agree on which émigré organization to support, they could not agree on how best to insert paramilitary army. The British supported amphibious landing while the US lobbies for low-level parachute drops. Ultimately, neither approach worked and in 1950, after a series of operational failures, the British finally walked away" (Corke S.-J., US Covert Operations and Cold War Strategy: Truman, Secret Warfare and the CIA, 1945-53, Abingdom, Routledge, 2008, p. 97).

[47]   See Miscamble W.D., George F. Kennan and the Making of American Foreign Policy, 1947-1950, cit., pp. 106-107.

1.4. **Process of adaptation**

The first CIA director was Admiral Roscoe Hillenkoetter, succeeding Vandenberg as the director of the CIG. Hillenkoetter immediately assumed a critical distance towards covert operations, believing that they would lead to an excessive exposure of the CIA and that, therefore, they could impair its analysis and information collection. Hillenkoetter also believed that in the National Security Act there was no provision authorizing the commitment of the agency in the field of clandestine operations.

This position costed Hillenkoetter a strong unpopularity and an accuse of weakness towards communism and the threat posed by Russia. The first estimates developed by the CIA were used by Hillenkoetter's detractors to support their criticisms. In fact, the quality of these reports was generally very high. Of a relatively liberal and reformist orientation concerning the policies that the United States should have supported and promoted abroad, these estimates often emphasized the Soviet weakness, highlighting the defensive nature of many of the international behaviors of the USSR. The analytical component of the CIA was immediately characterized as the more "far left" structure within the executive of the United States[48].

At the end of 1949, two events seemed to be able to change the course of the Cold War in favor of the USSR: the explosion of the first Soviet atomic bomb and the Communist victory in the Chinese civil war of Mao. The area controlled by international communism, considered by the United States government as a cohesive and monolithic block, now extended even to China. At the same time, the United States nuclear monopoly, which until then had been the main counterweight to the conventional military superiority of the communist bloc, met its own end.

These events generated a strong reaction in the United States, resulting in the search for culprits and scapegoats responsible for the "loss of China" and the acquisition of atomic secrets from the Soviets. For what concerns the second aspect, it was learned that the Soviet atomic program had benefited from the information provided by several spies that Moscow had managed to infiltrate in the American and British governments, as well as within the same nuclear laboratories at Los Alamos.

---

[48]   On Hillenkoetter: see Barrett D.M., The Cia And Congress: The Untold Story From Truman To Kennedy. Lawrence, University Press of Kansas, 2005; Kihss P., Adm. Roscoe H. Hillenkoetter, First Director of the C.I.A., "The New York Times", June 21, 1982.

The criticisms were directed especially at the intelligence services. Being, at least formally, the guide and the coordinator of these services, the CIA suddenly found itself at the center of a controversy. The main criticism moved to Hillenkoetter was that he had not foreseen the explosion of the Soviet atomic bomb. The estimates of the CIA, in fact, had not expected it before 1951[49].

Hillenkoetter therefore found himself attacked from many sides, and the outbreak of the Korean War provided the final pretext for his removal[50].

The story of the dismissal of Hillenkoetter was significant for several reasons. The first director of the CIA claimed that an excessive commitment of the agency in the field of covert operations could damage his reputation and impair

---

[49] "In the area of foreign policy, the United States faced major setbacks when the Soviet Union exploded its first atomic bomb on 29 August 1949, ending the U.S. monopoly. On 21 December 1949 Chiang Kai-shek was forced to leave mainland China for Taiwan by the communist forces led by Mao Zedong. These developments were seen as defeats by Republican critics who blamed communist sympathizers within the government, particularly the State Department" (Wynn N.A., The A to Z of the Roosevelt-Truman Era, Lanham, Rowman & Littlefield Publishing, 2008, p. 398). On these events: see also Hillstrom K., The Cold War, Detroit, Omnigraphics, 2006.

[50] "The Korean War was a conflict over two prizes: first, political control of Korea; and second, power in east Asia and the world as a whole. Historically, Communists and rightwing Nationalists vied for political control of Korea. Following the Second World War, the Communists gained control of North Korea and rightists gained control of South Korea. Both then wanted to unify the entire peninsula under their respective authority. This was what motivated North Korea to invade South Korea in June 1950. However Korea was also an object of Cold War superpower competition" (Malkasian C., The Korean War, New York, The Rosen Publishing Group, 2009, p. 5.

his analytical capacity. A failed operation, in fact, always left some aftermath: becoming public, it could be used propagandistically against the United States, exposing the network of field agents who had taken part in it, and could embarrass the administration that had implicitly organized it.

In addition, during his three years as director, Hillenkoetter was committed to promote the quality of the estimates developed by the CIA, transferring to the new agency most of the men working at the "research and analysis" of the OSS.

With respect to these objectives, the results obtained by Hillenkoetter underlined its political weakness. Against his will, the period between 1947 and 1950 was characterized by the strengthening of the operational component of the CIA, who enjoyed a considerable autonomy, although it was also torn by internal conflicts and overlapping responsibilities. In addition, the CIA had continued to have a rather weak status within the administration, which made it exposed to many attacks and criticisms[51].

In 1950, Walter Bedell Smith succeeded Hillenkoetter. Main contributor to Eisenhower during World War II and the

---

[51] "In fairness to Hillekoetter, he labored under the difficulty of serving during a period of continuing disagreement between Secretary of State Dean G. Acheson and Secretary of Defense Louis A. Johnson. With the Agency having to execute covert operations which were to serve the policy needs of the two Departments, the antagonism between the two Secretaries left the DCI in a difficult position" (Leary W.M., The Central Intelligence Agency, History and Documents, University of Alabama Press, 1984, p. 23).

American ambassador in Moscow from 1946 to 1949, Smith had the prestige and contacts that his predecessor had lacked. In order to strengthen the CIA, Smith chose two instruments: he began to employ qualified and respected collaborators, and promoted a radical reorganization of the agency.

Smith appointed as his deputy William Jackson, one of the leading experts in intelligence in the United States, and brought into the agency Allen Dulles, the legendary head of the OSS station in Bern as well as the brother of John Foster, the future Secretary of State for Eisenhower. While Jackson was in the CIA for only a few months, Dulles would replace Smith in 1953, remaining at the head of the agency for more than eight years and becoming one of the most powerful and influential directors in its history.

The internal reforms promoted by Smith sought to eliminate the many conflicts of jurisdiction still present within the CIA, and ensure greater importance to estimates prepared by the central intelligence. To reach this goal, Smith wanted that the large production of information material should be condensed into a single summary report to be presented to President Truman[52].

---

[52] On Smith: see Crosswell D.K.R., Beetle: The Life of General Walter Bedell Smith, University Press of Kentucky, 2010; Montague L.L., General Walter Bedell Smith as Director of Central Intelligence, October 1950 - February 1953, The Pennsylvania University Press, 1992.

The responsibilities of this job evaluation and synthesis was assigned to a new body, renamed Office of National Estimates (ONE), whose head was William Langer (Harvard University historian)[53].

At the same time, Smith began a process of elimination of duplicates inside the CIA, bringing together the various parts of the analytical component of the CIA within a single structure called the Directorate of Intelligence (DDI).

A similar process was promoted within the operational component. Smith in fact put an end to the anomaly represented by the OPC, as on one hand it drew from the budget of the CIA while the manager was appointed by the Secretary of State. Smith then brought the director under his control.

Smith also intervened on the antagonism between the OPC and OSO (the old structure of the CIG responsible for covert operations) that, with the birth of the CIA, had dealt mainly with espionage and counter-espionage. Formally, the OPC was to promote covert operations, while the OSO was

---

[53]   "Acquiring solid intelligence and producing estimates was a key challenge for the CIA, and Smith pressed for the development of coordinated intelligence analysis and the precise use of language for estimates. He used the expression 'war is possible' to illustrate its importance [...]. U.S. policy makers needed independent estimates, and the CIA was the logical agency to produce them. The founding director of the Board (later Office) of National Estimates was the Harvard historian William L. Langer" (Brugioni D.A., Eyes in the Sky: Eisenhower, the CIA, and Cold War Aerial Espionage, Annapolis, Naval Institute Press, 2010, p. 38).

responsible for the collection of secret information. In fact, the distinction between the two tasks was not so defined, so much so, that both offices could make use of the same agents.

At first, Smith thought he could put an end to this situation by appointing his Deputy Director Allen Dulles responsible OSO and OPC. To Dulles, which advocated a merger of the operational components of the CIA, was assigned the responsibility to promote the coordination of the two structures that retained though their autonomy. Seeing that the attempts to force OSO and OPC to collaborate resulted useless, Smith opted for the drastic solution of unifying them in an ancient structure creating, in August 1952, the Directorate of Plans (DDP). The reorganization process was completed by the institution of a third and final directorate, the Directorate of Administration (DDA), which was assigned to administrative duties and those relating to logistical support for operations abroad[54].

Smith's reforms created the institutional skeleton of the CIA, which lasted for more than two decades. These strengthened the agency and laid the foundations for the

---

[54]   See Johnson L.K., Strategic Intelligence, Westport, Preager Security International, 2007, vol. 3, p. 162.

period of great splendor that the CIA reached under the direction of Allen Dulles (1953-1962) [55].

The organizational centralization removed many of the situations of dualism and overlapping of jurisdictions inside the American Central Intelligence Agency. The involvement of figures of great prestige meant that to this increased efficiency also corresponded an increasing of the status and recognition within the administration.

Smith's new course was not able though to stop the increasing efforts in the field of CIA covert operations that the new director, like his predecessor, regarded with the same annoyance. At the beginning of 1953, when Smith left the direction of the CIA to become Secretary of State, more than 60% of the agency's personnel was employed by the operational component (DDP). The same fusion between OSO and OPC had resolved, basically, the "conquest" of the

---

[55]   "Smith possessed the authority to build a structure in keeping with his own ideas on how a centralized bureaucracy should operate. His predecessors never overcame the inherent frictions the intelligence agency faces in dealing with the armed services, the FBI, and the State Department; as the CIA rapidly expanded, it became a bureaucratic morass of competing interests [...]. The structure he eventually put in place mirrored his wartime thinking" (Crosswell D.K.R., Beetle: The Life of General Walter Bedell Smith, cit., pp. 221-222).

latter by the former, and hence with the assertion of the more unscrupulous and dynamic "operational arms" of the CIA[56].

Finally, Dulles had proclaimed to be a supporter of covert operations, conflicting often with Smith for this reason.

The prestige and efficiency acquired by the CIA were the essential prerequisites for the period of great success that characterized the work of the agency under Dulles' direction. These years, however, were also characterized by further intensification of its clandestine operations abroad, so as to be called "the golden age of the covert operations".

For many, including Dulles, the effectiveness of the intelligence service was evaluated on the basis of clandestine operations undertaken and of the outcomes achieved in the short term. Some of the worst excesses of the operational component of the CIA, which would have undermined the image and prestige for many years to come, date back to these years[57].

---

[56]   "The 'fusion' of the old OPC and OSO Doolittle termed a 'shotgun' marriage. The report warned that the 'Cold War functions' of the Directorate for Operations overshadowed its espionage role, and the committee recommended the DO be reorganized into a viable 'Cold War shop'" (Prados J., Safe for Democracy: The Secret Wars of the CIA, Chicago, Ivan R. Dee, 2006, p. 149).

[57]   On Dulles: see Dulles A., The Craft of Intelligence: America's Legendary Spy Master on the Fundamentals of Intelligence Gathering for a Free World, Washington,Lion Press, 2006; Srode J., Allen Dulles: Master of Spies, Washington, Regnery Publishing, 1999; Grose P., Gentleman Spy: The Life of Allen Dulles, University of Massachusetts Press, 1996.

CHAPTER 2

THE MISSIONS IN OTHER COUNTRIES

2.0. Introduction

During the Fifties, the CIA continued its clandestine activities in Europe. The main aim of the United States was to consolidate the Western bloc and prevent possible access to power by the communist parties, especially the Italian and French ones. Between 1951 and 1952, the United States drew up anticommunist action plans in Italy and France, which they assigned code names of *Demagnetize* and *Cloven* (later called *Clydesdale* and *Midiron*). These plans called for a series of measures, headed under the category of "psychological warfare", such as the requisition of ex-fascists buildings from the PCI at the end of the war (that were turned into People's Houses), the anti-communist propaganda and disinformation, financial and organizational support to non-communist trade unions and pro-Western associations such as "Peace and freedom", and the penetration inside of communist organizations with the ultimate aim to destabilize them, fueling internal divisions[58].

Demagnetize and *Cloven* were processed and managed by a body set up in 1951, the Psychological Strategy Board (PSB), who included the State Department of Defense, the ACIA and the Mutual Security Agency (MSA). To the PSB were assigned the tasks of planning and coordination, while the operational responsibility was largely delegated to the governments of the two countries. The De Gasperi government refused, however, to put into practice the measures provided for by the plans, thus causing irritation in the American ally. The substantial failure of the plans of "psychological warfare" promoted by the United States in Italy and in France was also caused, though, by the lack of consensus within the PSB concerning on which lines promoting and supporting

---

[58] "These plans thus dealt with a variety of issues, but the main thrust of the PSB remained to maneuver French and Italian nationalism, or at least to stifle Communist attempts of exploring nationalist feelings. The 1951 electoral tests underscored and obvious nationalist turn in both France and Italy. This made French and Italian governments more jealous than usual of their sovereignty [...]. This caution had to be applied to all PSB campaigns, from the most innocent ones to the repressive measures of 'Cloven' and 'Demagnetize'" (Brogi A., A question of Self-Esteem: The United States and the Cold War Choices in France and Italy, 1944-1958, Westport, Praeger Publisher, 2002, p. 141).

the local stakeholders. The activity of the PSB was marked by clashes between its members and the State Department's refusal to cede some of their skills on the same PSB[59].

The main unofficial activity promoted by the CIA in Western Europe continued to be the financing of pro-Atlantic political parties and trade unions, as the Italian CISL. The intervention of the United States, and then the CIA, in the Italian elections of 1953, for example, was much more limited than it was in 1948 for fear that it could produce counterproductive effects[60].

The crystallization of the bipolar division of the continent and the process of decolonization resulted from the gradual disintegration of European colonial powers were moving the competition between the United States and the Soviet Union to theaters that until then had remained extraneous.

---

[59] "The Truman administration approved eighty-one covert operations during this period, few of them with more than cursory input form the Psychological Strategy Board [...]. Evidence indicates that the Psychological Strategy Board failed as the U.S. high command for covert action due to the opposition of the line agencies [...]. The close relationship between psychological warfare and covert operations is further demonstrated by what happened to U.S. programs. Rather than restraining and coordinating propaganda and covert activities, the Psychological Strategy Board that Harry Truman created instead became a stimulant for an intensification of the Cold War" (Prados J., Safe for Democracy: The Secret Wars of the CIA, cit., p. 82).

[60] Brogi A., A question of Self-Esteem: The United States and the Cold War Choices in France and Italy, 1944-1958, cit., p. 143.

Therefore, even the covert operations began to be directed towards these new areas of crisis.

The two most famous covert operations promoted by the CIA in the fifties (*Ajax* and *Pbsuccess*) were put in place in Iran and Guatemala. In spite of the obvious diversity and their geographical remoteness, for the United States there were important elements of affinity between these two countries. In both, there were strong western economic interests to defend, represented by British and American multinational capitals (Anglo-Iranian Oil Company in Iran and the United Fruit Company in Guatemala) operating in a state of monopolistic advantage that could have been jeopardized by the evolution of the domestic political context.

These interests also intertwined with the fear that the Soviet Union could benefit from a situation of instability, emerged in the two countries, to expand their influence in areas (the Middle East and Latin America) considered strategically vital to American security.

2.1 The *Ajax* and the *Pbsuccess* operations

2.1.1. *The Ajax operation in Iran*

In Iran, the plans of Prime Minister Mossadegh for the nationalization of the oil wells managed by the Anglo-Iranian Oil Company, threatened the Western control over resources in the Middle East, representing a dangerous precedent that other regional leaders could follow, and threatened to create a rapprochement between Iran and Soviet Union. For this reason, the Eisenhower administration decided to promote a clandestine operation aimed at convincing the young Iranian monarch Rezha Palevi to remove Mossadegh from his office, replacing him with the more moderate and pro-Western Fazlollah Zahedi[61].

The covert CIA operation in Iran was based on two main elements:

1. mobilization (through substantial funding) for groups of Zahedi supporters, who were supposed to lead demonstrations and riots in Tehran, forcing Mossadegh to resign;

---

[61]   See Smith W.T., Encyclopedia of the Central Intelligence Agency, cit., p. 13.

2. the U.S. commitment to reward Rezha Palevi's regime with economic and military aid.

The CIA's operation achieved the desired results, in spite of the superficiality and dilettantism with which it was conducted. Mossadegh resigned in August 1953 after several days of hard street clashes between his supporters and those of Zahedi, which caused more than 300 deaths[62].

Rezha Palevi appointed Zahedi prime minister. The Anglo-Iranian Oil Company was forced to give up their monopoly to split the huge Iranian oil resources with some large U.S. companies (the Gulf, New Jersey Standard, Texaco and Socony-Mobil), which obtained a participation of 40 % in their management[63].

It remains to determine at what extent the intervention of the CIA was really decisive. Likely, it had, at most, the effect of reinforcing trends already in place: the Mossadegh government was very precarious and its survival was linked

---

[62]   Ibidem.

[63]   In the D'Agostino's opinion, "the increased royalties did not satisfy Iranian nationalists, especially since the revenues were enriching the local ruling class to the neglect of the people. In 1951, the country's parliament nationalized the oil industry. In response, the Eisenhower administration approved a CIA covert operation two years later to remove the democratically elected prime minister, Mohammad Mossadeq" (D'Agostino B., The Middle Class Fights Back: How Progressiv Movements Can Restore Democracy in America, Santa Barbara, ABC-Clio, 2012, p. 20).

to a number of factors (including the willingness of Palevi) that could fail in the absence of U.S. pressure.

The success achieved in Iran, however, fueled the enthusiasm of Eisenhower's administrate concerning covert operations. A few months later, the United States decided to promote a new clandestine operation, this time against the democratic government of Jacobo Arbenz in Guatemala.

2.1.2. *The Pbsuccess operation in Guatemala*

The Guatemalan army officer Jacobo Arbenz, of a clearly socialist orientation, was elected president in 1951. Among his first acts there was the legalization of the little Communist Party of Guatemala (which had about 5000 subscribers), this way causing concern and irritation in the United States.

The Arbenz government had also implemented a land reform aimed at redistributing land ownership to small and medium farmers. The U.S. hostility against Arbenz was primarily due to the fact that the reform struck the main U.S. company operating in the country, i.e. the United Fruit Company (dubbed the "octopus" because of the influence and weight who exercised in the society and politics of Guatemala).

The Truman administration had resisted the demands of the United Fruit to intervene so to put an end to Arbenz's reforms. Eisenhower and John Foster Dulles took instead a decision aimed at thwarting the spread of socialist ideas in the American continent and to protect U.S. interests in the region. Once again, therefore, the choice of the U.S. of intervening in the internal affairs of another state was dictated by a complex interplay of ideological bias, economic motivations, and strategic considerations (and the fear of a possible extension of the Soviet influence in Latin America).

Opposed by many officials in the State Department and the CIA itself, the covert operation carried out in Guatemala (*Pbsuccess*) provided for the support of opponents of Arbenz in Guatemala's armed forces, training in Florida with a group of Guatemalan dissidents, who were supposed to return in the country, and the promotion of a campaign of radio propaganda.

The action of the exiles, which in fact corresponded to an invasion of the country, would be presented as part of a spontaneous popular uprising against Arbenz. The prediction, then proven correct, was that the Guatemalan president would ultimately succumb, leaving the country[64].

The operation was put in place in June 1954 when several hundred paramilitaries (with the support of a few air units made available by the CIA) penetrated the inland of Guatemala. It was a premise, designed to lay the foundations of the political destabilization of the country, but that was

---

[64]   Smith W.T., Encyclopedia of the Central Intelligence Agency, cit., p. 230.

enough to induce Albenz to flee abroad. In his place, Colonel Carlos Castillo Armas took office, abrogating the agricultural reform and establishing a brutal military dictatorship.

Ironically, the United Fruit was not able to benefit from the change of regime. Subject to antitrust investigation by the U.S., it was forced to give up the dominant position held until then in Guatemala[65].

2.1.3. *Ajax and Pbsuccess: a first evaluation*

The covert operations promoted in Iran and Guatemala reflected the gradual globalization of the strategy of containment and U.S. progressive inability to deal with local situations not conformed with the dichotomous logic that characterized the Cold War and the bipolar US-URSS antagonism. It is hard to believe that in Iran and Guatemala there was a real danger for the spread of communism, and that Mossadegh and Arbenz represented threats to the national security of the United States. Economic interests and a blind anticommunism often led, however, to promote actions

---

[65] On the events in Guatelama, see Immermann R.H., The CIA in Guatemala: The Foreign Policy of Intervention, University of Texas Press, 2010; Manweller M., Chronology of the U.S. Presidency, Santa Barbara, ABC-Clio, 2012, p. 1076.

destined to bring serious repercussions in the long term[66]: it became more and more frequent the tendency to abandon the strategy of social, political and economic reforms as tools to stop the spreading of communism, in favor of interventions that seemed capable of providing immediate results and at low cost.

The success of these operations, however, led to overestimate their effectiveness and universal applicability. The importance attached to these instruments by the Eisenhower administration, and the belief that any means was legitimate to contain the spreading of communism further strengthened the operational component of the CIA, fueling an internal sense of omnipotence and strengthening it against the analytical component.

Ajax and *Pbsuccess* operations had been authorized by the White House but, inevitably, their implementation was

---

[66]   "For the next quarter century, the increasingly dictatorial Shah Reza Pahlavi ruled Iran, with support of the United States and a secret police notorious for its involvement in torture. The shah not only granted favorable concession to big U.S. oil companies, but also, like the Saudis, used a large portion of his country's share of the oil money to buy expensive weapons systems from U.S. defense contractors" (D'Agostino B., The Middle Class Fights Back: How Progressiv Movements Can Restore Democracy in America, cit., p. 20).

marked by confusion and the need to leave to the absolute discretion of the agents operating in those countries[67].

The effectiveness of covert operations depended on their secrecy and lack of binding mechanisms they were supposed to follow. At the same time, the need to avoid that the responsibility of any failures of the operations promoted by the CIA would fall back on the White House required to minimize contacts between the latter and those who ran the operation, avoiding the identification of an explicit presidential authorization of the action. This gave further autonomy and independence to CIA's operatives, laying the foundations for the excesses and the degeneration that characterized their activities in subsequent years. At this point there was a tendency to consider the vague directions from the executive

---

[67] "President Eisenhower and Secretary Dulles wanted to protect the image of the United States abroad, particularly in Latin America. Just a few weeks before Eisenhower assumed the presidency, a CIA National Intelligence Estimate had stressed that Latin America was threatened by 'the pressure of exaggerated nationalism' and that this trend might eventually 'affect Hemispheric solidarity and U.S. security interests' [...]. Thus, there were 'a paradox at the heart of PBSUCCESS', a paradox that was resolved by a figleaf. 'The figleaf was designed to deny U.S. involvement [...] yet the success of the operation hinged on convincing the Guatemalans that the U.S. was indeed involved'" (Gleijeses P., Shattered Hope: The Guatemalan Revolution and the United States, 1944-1954, Princeton University Press, 1991, p. 247).

as an implicit permission to promote action that were not subjected to the necessary forms of control and supervision[68].

The results of the success of *Ajax* and *Pbsuccess* were very different from those anticipated and desired. In the name of anticommunism, the United States came to attach their names to authoritarian regimes, thwarting the same CIA's propaganda efforts to counter the widespread anti-Americanism.

Rezha Palevi proved to be not the liberal and enlightened monarch the United States had hoped for, even though he proved to be a loyal ally for the United States in the Middle East until the theocratic revolution of 1979 and the advent of Khomeini.

In Guatemala, the U.S. supported a murderous and dictatorial regime, ending to train in their military academies officers that would plan and perpetrate the slaughter of tens of thousands of Guatemalan famers.

---

[68] "Proceeding on the premise that the army was the ultimate arbiter of Guatemala's political order, the objective of PBSUCCESS was to introduce the military's chief officers to abandon Arbenz in favor of a counterrevolutionary regime. The CIA strategy in Iran had been to buttress bribery with psychological warfare. The CIA reversed the equation in Guatemala ad added assassination as a variable to hold in reserve" (Theoharis A.G., The Central Intelligence Agency: Security Under Scrutiny, Westport, Greenwood Press, 2006, p. 26).

2.2. **Decline of the CIA**

The importance given by the Eisenhower administration to covert operations, the quality of intelligence produced and the political weight of Allen Dulles had contributed significantly to enhance the status and importance of the CIA within the executive[69]. During the Fifties, as mentioned, there was anyway a great criticism that would expose the subjectivity and the alleged inefficiency of intelligence's central agenda.

To quieten the demands of subjecting the activities of the CIA to stricter controls, Eisenhower established the *ad hoc* committees, responsible for submitting the agency to the necessary checks outside of the Congress.

In 1954 a special commission headed by Air Force General James Doolittle was established. The final report was very critical especially of the work of director Allen Dulles, who was accused of not being able to coordinate the work of the agency with those of other intelligence in the United States and being an administrator incapable to manage and control his

---

[69]   "With the onset of the Cold War, the CIA quickly took on a life of its own, gaining over time an increased level of autonomy, funding and jurisdiction. The requirement for intelligence on the Soviet Union, its allies and suspected communist subversion, using more sophisticated methods, became of supreme importance to the US government. By the early 1950s, the CIA was actively involved in subversive activities. More important, the agency had also taken on increased responsibility for the collection of intelligence" (Bury E., Eisenhower and the Cold War Arm Race, London, Tauris & Co., 2014, p. 133)

subordinates. The report also expressed concern with regard to the fact that between the CIA director and the secretary of state there was a kind of bond (called "inappropriate")[70].

A few months later, two authoritative representatives of the establishment of the United States (graduates Robert Lovett and David Bruce) moved even more severe criticism against the CIA and in particular its operational component. Bruce and Lovett were negatively impressed by the amount of people and resources that the CIA undertook in the field of covert operations and especially by the fact that many of them constitute flagrant violations of national sovereignty of countries in which they took place.

The attack of Bruce and Lovett was unprecedented. The way in which CIA authorized and ran covert operations were severely criticized. Their report illustrated clearly the superficiality of many covert operations, the lack of control

---

[70]   "On 30 September 1954, Doolittle submitted his sixty-page classified report directly to Eisenhower [...]. This report addressed the need to professionalize intelligence, including several recommendations calling for more efficient, internal administration, including recruitment and training procedures, background checks of personnel, and the need to correct the natural tendency to over classify documents originating in the agency. It also called for increased cooperation between the clandestine and analytical sides of the agency" (Goldman J., Ethics of Spying: A Reader for the Intelligence Professional, Plymouth, Scarecrow Press, 2010, pp. 19-20).

bindings, and the absolute subjectivity left at those operating in the field[71].

The report denounced the prevailing mentality of the CIA, based on an activism often unnecessary and poorly attentive to the possible consequences. Its agents, in fact, were often forced to demonstrate to do something to justify their existence.

The invitation of Bruce and Lovett to make a more limited use of covert operations by making more strict the criteria by which they were planned and authorized, was not very successful, especially for the fact that Eisenhower continued to defend Dulles, whom he considered one of his more capable and reliable counselors. For this reason, Dulles remained firmly in place until two high profile failures of the CIA (the shooting down of the U-2 spy plane and the failure of

---

[71]   "The Bruce-Lovett Report was a critical appraisal of the Central Intelligence Agency's (CIA) proliferation of covert operations during the early years of the cold war [...]. The report condemned what Bruce and Lovett viewed as the subordination of official US policy to covert policy initiatives" (Bentley D.A., Bruce-Lovett Report, in Hastedt G.P. ed., Spies, Wiretaps, and Secret Operations, Santa Barbara, ABC-Clio, 2011, p. 109).

the landing at the Bay of Pigs) marked the beginning of his downward spiral[72].

The flights of the U-2 aircraft started in 1956 and continued in subsequent years. Their purpose was photographic espionage, one of the most important projects implemented by the CIA[73].

These missions had two opposite consequences. On one hand there were those who, seeing that the progress made by the USSR in the field of missile and radar technology made these flights increasingly dangerous, believed that the time had come to put an end to such flights. On the other hand, John Kennedy and the Democratic Party pushed Eisenhower to authorize a new series of U-2 missions. The result was that the number of flights of these aircraft scheduled for April 1960 were postponed for one month: in April, in fact, a summit of the leaders of the United States, Soviet Union, Britain and France was to be held in Paris, and Eisenhower wanted to avoid a possible accident before that meeting. The

---

[72] "Because Eisenhower and Dulles believed that rhetorical diplomacy best served their goal of achieving a globalist consensus, they continued to use excessive rhetoric as a strategic, diplomatic tool. But when it came time to bite the bullet and implement their confidential strategies of competitive coexistence with the Soviet Union and alliance management with the allies, they could not break out of the public, rhetorical traps they had created. Thus the ideology of Eisenhower administration's public anti-communism in international diplomacy mattered greatly" (Tudda C., The Truth is Our Weapon: The Rhetorical Diplomacy of Dwight D. Eisenhower and John Foster Dulles, Louisiana University Press, 2006, p. 128).

[73] Bury E., Eisenhower and the Cold War Arm Race, cit., pp. 67-68.

Paris summit was of utmost importance as the year before Khrushchev had made a trip to the United States to lay the foundations of a thaw in US-Soviet relations and a general improvement of international relations; these intentions would have to be confirmed in Paris[74].

Back to the U-2, on May 1st 1960, a plane flown by Gary Powers took off from Peshawar in Pakistan to photograph the Soviet missile base Tyuratam in Kazakhstan, was shot down by the Soviet Union. Once verified the shooting down, the CIA put into action the expected covering plan: the flights of the U-2, which had been formally placed under the newborn U.S. space agency (National Aeronautics and Space Administration—NASA), were to be presented as part of a program of scientific and meteorological studies.

Benefiting also from the support of a rather benign press, the announcement of the retention of U-2 shot down by the Soviets did not attract much attention[75]. Later, however, also

---

[74] "From 1953 to early 1955, Eisenhower had consistently take in line that fruitful negotiations with the Soviet Union would not be possible until a security union for Western Europe had been achieved. By the early spring of 1955, all the signatory countries had ratified the Paris Agreements [...]. Eisenhower adopted an overall cautious approach towards summit talks" (Bury E., Eisenhower and the Cold War Arm Race, cit., p. 84).

[75] The front plan was based on two essential conditions, which were guaranteed by Eisenhower when he authorized the program: the pilot would not have survived the shoot down of the aircraft and the latter would be completely destroyed. In reality, however, Powers was captured alive by the Soviets, who also recovered some pieces of U-2 (see Marrs J., Crossfire: The Plot who Killed Kennedy, New York, Basic Books, 2010, p. 120).

because of the growing international turmoil, the USSR made known the truth about the incident, causing a strong reaction from the United States. This fact had strong repercussions on the meeting in Paris, contributing to the deterioration of relations between the U.S. and the USSR. To these events was also added the so-called "Cuba affair".

2.3. The Cuba " affair"

On the island of Cuba, in January 1959, the dictatorship of Batista Fulgentio was overthrown by a revolutionary movement led by Fidel Castro, who had formed a coalition government.

The U.S. hostility against the new Cuban government and the Soviet availability to provide economic aid to Cuba caused the moving to the left of Castro, who took increasingly radical, closer to Russia positions.

From their side, the United States did not accept that a state of the American continent could become communist because it would have constituted a dangerous precedent and would have favored the extension of Soviet influence in the western hemisphere too.

To avoid this, Eisenhower decided to resort once again to a covert operation based on the model of *Pbsuccess* in Guatemala. The CIA then formed a task force with the task of planning and managing a clandestine operation aimed at overthrowing the Castro regime. The original plans provided only for acts of sabotage against Cuban industrial plants, but soon gave way to a much more ambitious plan[76].

This covert operation, which also included bizarre plans to assassinate Castro, was inherited by the new U.S. President John Fitzgerald Kennedy, who was elected in November 1960 after defeating by a few votes the Republican candidate Richard Nixon[77].

As it already happened on other occasions, this covert operation was organized by the CIA in an independent and uncontrollable way, despite the fact that Kennedy administration had raised several doubts about it.

Against the advice of some of his co-workers (including the economist John Kenneth Galbraith, then ambassador in

---

[76]   "On January 18, 1960, the CIA set up a special task force composed mainly of veterans of the 1954 intervention against the Arbenz government in Guatemala. This task force prepared a wide-ranging attack on the Castro regime [...]. Finally, on March 16, 1960, a systematic plan of covert action against the Castro regime was put into place and presented to Eisenhower for approval" (Farber S., The Origins of the Cuban Revolution Reconsidered, University of North Carolina Press, 2006, p. 84).

[77]   This project, which was adopted in March 1960, included four key elements: 1. the creation of a political organization formed by moderate and anti-Castro Cuban exiles in the United States; 2. the activation of a radio station for propaganda; 3. the construction of a network of agents in Cuba; 4. the establishment and training of a brigade composed of anti-Castro Cubans to be entrusted with the responsibility of the paramilitary aspects of the operation (see Ciment J., Hill K., Encyclopedia of Conflict Since World War II, Abingdom, Routledge, 1999, pp. 508-509).

India), the elected president of the United States had confirmed at his place as the head of the CIA Allen Dulles and J. Edgar Hoover as FBI director. The new administration was keen to downplay the role of the CIA in favor of the Intelligence Service of the Department of State (Bureau of Intelligence and Research—INR) directed by Roger Hilsman, a leading intelligence experts in all the Member States[78].

Kennedy agreed that the operation on Cuba would continue because he had misunderstood the manner in which it was conducted. The President, in fact, believed that the operation consisted mainly in the infiltration of anti-Castro agents in Cuba and that the expected landing of the Cuban brigade responded to this aim. For the CIA, however, the intervention in Cuba should have been a mission of grand style, backed also by some U.S. planes flown by Cubans. Allen Dulles was convinced that, in case of the difficulties would arise, Kennedy would have agreed to involve even the U.S. army. Within the CIA, in fact, thanks to the success of previous covert operations, there was the firm belief that not even the President's opinion could limit their actions.

In April 17th 1961, the Cuban brigade made of approximately 1,400 men, landed in the Bay of Pigs. Contrary

---

[78]   See Kaiser D.E., American Tragedy: Kennedy, Johnson, and the Origins of the Vietnam War, Harvard University Press, 2000, p. 153.

to expectations, it had to face a stiff resistance from the Castro's armed forces, and was hit by the bombings of three Cuban aviation aircraft. In the face of imminent defeat, Kennedy refused to send in the army, causing the indignation of Dulles. The anti-Castro Cubans were quickly defeated and the expected internal insurrection was not organized. At the same time, as had already happened in the case of U-2, the coverage of the CIA did not survive and the affair became public.

2.4. **Other covert operations**

The episode of the Bay of Pigs constituted another defeat for the image of the United States. Impeached, the CIA and its director found themselves totally marginalized within the executive.

This situation took a decisive turn in the fall of 1961, when Kennedy decided to replace Allen Dulles. After evaluating the possibility of appointing his brother Robert, the President chose as the new director a Californian businessman, John McCone. McCone was a Republican with solid anti-communist credentials and had already worked with the

Eisenhower administration as chairman of the Atomic Energy Commission[79].

The progress made by the CIA under the direction of McCone enabled the United States to obtain information on Soviet missile technology and to monitor USSR compliance to the Agreement of 1963, which banned nuclear tests in the atmosphere.

McCone's "theoretical" committment, however, did not reflect the intentions of the Kennedy administration in relation to covert operations which, according to the presidency, had yet to achieve a central role in the United States foreign policy.

This policy implied a greater presence of President's trustworthy men in the appropriate special groups responsible for the supervision of the CIA, and an innovative intensification of covert operations[80]. For example, the effort to overthrow Castro continued even after the episode of the Bay of Pigs. In

---

[79]   McCone promoted a restructuring to improve the analytical capacity of the agency. His reforms focused mainly on the crucial transition between the time the information was collected and that of their preparation and processing, which in the past had been the basis of many of the misunderstandings and judgmental mistakes made by the CIA. The main aim of McCone was to raise the quality of the estimates presented by the CIA to the presidency, so that the CIA regained credibility and trust (Blight J.G., Velch D.A., Intelligence and the Cuban Missile Crisis, Abingdom, Routledge, 2013, pp. 132-133).

[80]   Blight J.G., Velch D.A., Intelligence and the Cuban Missile Crisis, cit., p. 133.

November 1961, in fact, was adopted a program of measures against the Cuban leader, named *Mongoose* operation[81].

The programs for the assassination of foreign leaders were not limited to Castro, but were also drawn against the Congolese leader Patrick Lumumba (the killing, however, was not the work of the CIA), and the American intelligence services actively encouraged coups in South Vietnam and in the Dominican Republic, which led to the death of the two dictators Rafael Trujillo and Diem Ngo Dihn.

Clandestine operations on a large scale were promoted in Laos against the Pathet Lao movement, which supported the communist regime of North Vietnam, and Latin America, where the increasing marginalization of the most progressive members of the Kennedy administration corresponded to an increased willingness to abandon the democratic reformist strategy initially adopted by Kennedy in favor of more traditional means of fighting communism.

The covert operations sponsored by the CIA in the Western Hemisphere, ranged from financial and organizational support towards the political forces and non-communist

---

[81] "One development in this period, not (presumably) known to the Soviet leaders, nor for that matter to any but a very few American leaders, was a series of continuing meetings of the secret Special Group (Augmented) that had been established in November 1961 to conduct covert operations against Cuba under the code-name 'Mongoose'. Attorney General Kennedy was a driving force in this covert action program" (Farthoff R.L., Reflections on the Cuban Missile Crisis, Washington, Brookings Institution Press, 1989, p. 32).

trade union, to actual destabilization, like the one fueled by the CIA against the democratically elected leaders of British Guyana and Ecuador, respectively Jose Velasco Ibarra[82] and Cheddi Jagan[83].

---

[82] "In September 1960, a new government headed by José María Velasco Ibarra came to power.. Velasco had won a decisive electoral victory, running on a vaguely liberal, populist, something-for-everyone platform. He was no Fidel Castro, he was not even a socialist, but he earned the wrath of the US State Department and the CIA by his unyielding opposition to the two stated priorities of American policy in Ecuador: breaking relations with Cuba, and clamping down on activists of the Communist Party and those to their left. Over the next three years, in pursuit of those goals, the CIA left as little as possible to chance [...]. CIA-supported activities were carried out without the knowledge of the American ambassador [...]. Finally, in November 1961, the military acted. Velasco was forced to resign and replaced by Vice-President Carlos Julio Arosemana [...]. Arosemana soon proved no more acceptable to the CIA than Velasco. All operations continued, particularly the campaign to break relations with Cuba, which Arosemana steadfastly refused to do [...]. On 11 July 1963 the Presidential Palace in Quito was surrounded by tanks and troops. Arosemana was out, a junta was in. Their first act was to outlaw communism; 'communists' and other 'extreme' leftists were rounded up and jailed, the arrests campaign being facilitated by data from the CIA's Subversive Control Watch List [...]. Civil liberties were suspended; the 1964 elections canceled; another tale told many times in Latin America" (Blum W., Killing Hope: Military and CIA interventions Since World War II, London Zed Books, 2003, pp. 154-155).

[83] "In addition to the Chilean operations, the Kennedy administration also undertook, much to the astonishment of the British government, a long, determined campaign, diplomatically and covertly, to prevent the Marxist Chedi Jagan from becoming the head of government in British Guyana after it achieved independence. Professor John Lewis Gaddis notes that Jagan, as a Marxist, made no better impression than Castro and Kennedy ordered the CIA to get rid of him, believing that Jagan constituted a major threat to the region" (Daugherty W., Executive Secrets: Covert Action and the Presidency, Lexington, The University Press of Kentucky, 2004, p. 157).

2.5. In Vietnam: the " Secret Army"

To these series of covert operations also belongs the action organized during the Vietnam War. The American decision to intervene militarily to defend South Vietnam rested on the fact that in Indochina a global offensive from international communism was taking place, and by the fact that the U.S. had the means and resources to stop it. Both of these points, however, were openly contested by the estimates prepared by the CIA.

Among other beliefs, the CIA doubted the fact that behind North Vietnam and the Vietcong (the name with which were renamed the leaders of the national liberation movement operating in the south of the country) there were China and the Soviet Union. The CIA also expressed strong criticism of the Johnson administration's decision to implement a comprehensive and devastating plan of aerial bombing of North Vietnam (Operation Rolling Thunder)[84].

The presidency of the United States, however, chose to ignore the concerns of the CIA and the decision to deploy U.S.

---

[84] In this case also, the CIA denounced the uselessness of a substantially similar strategy because the bombings were thought unfit to deal with revolutionary movements and still had limited effect when used against still largely agricultural and underdeveloped countries like North Vietnam. This was the line of thought of the CIA throughout all phases of the air campaign the U.S. (1965-1968) (see Landers J., The Weekly War: Neswmagazines and Vietnam, University of Missouri Press, 2004, pp. 127-128).

ground troops to Vietnam was made by Johnson, although the premise of the intervention had already been placed by Kennedy during his presidency.

For the 1964-65 biennium the CIA was not asked for the preparation of any estimate on this aspect. On the other hand, the first pessimistic estimates about the possible success of a ground intervention, developed by the CIA under the direction of McCone, remained unheard by the Presidency. The greatest strength of the evaluations carried out by the CIA about the Vietnamese situation laid in the fact that the data considered were real and objective, while those in possession of military forces were not[85].

The process of "Vietnamization" of U.S. policy did not lead to any reduction in the commitment of CIA's operatives in the region. Elected to the presidency of the United States in 1969, Nixon's first mandate years were those of the operation *Phoenix* promoted by the CIA and the army, in order to make South Vietnam impervious to communist penetration. The dramatic results of the action (over 20,000 deaths) intertwined

---

[85]   "In spite of opposition, McCone remained CIA director after President Kennedy's November 1963 assassination. However, McCone may have initiated his own demise under President Lyndon B. Johnson by criticizing escalation of the war in Vietnam. Early on McCone noted that Operation Rolling Thunder, the bombing of North Vietnam, was not working and that escalation would fail because it could not change the odds" (Tucker S.C., The Encyclopedia of the Vietnam War, Santa Barbara, ABC-Clio, 2011, p. 717).

with those caused by CIA's interventionism, especially in Cambodia, where in March 1970 a military coup led to the death of Prince Sihanouk and the coming to power of Marshal Lon Nol. Sihanouk had assumed a position of neutrality in respect to the Vietnam War, which, however, tolerated the Vietcong "sanctuaries " in Cambodian territory. The prince accused the United States and the CIA of having planned and supported the coup. Although the direct involvement of the CIA was never proven, the American government backed Lon Nol in the name of anti-communism and contributed, albeit indirectly, into dragging Cambodia into a civil war that would lead to one of the craziest and most bloodthirsty dictatorship of the history: that of the Khmer Rouge of Pol Nol[86].

---

[86] "Operation Phoemix was a controversial special project in the Vietnam War when Vietcong leaders were identified by U.S. intelligence officers to be targeted by U.S. forces" (Smith W.T., Encyclopedia of the Central Intelligence Agency, cit., p. 188)

2.6. In Chile: the *Fubelt* operation

Among the most outstanding covert operations sponsored by the CIA during Nixon's presidency (1968-1974), there was one carried out in Chile. The goal of Nixon and Kissinger, in this country, was to avoid the excessive power of the socialist leader Salvador Allende. As was already the case in Latin America, U.S. diplomacy's action was backed by some powerful industrial groups of the United States (Telephone and Telegraph, IT & T), hostile to the nationalization program supported by Allende.

The covert operations supported by the United States in Chile were initially represented by the provision of financial aid to the Christian Democrats and the conservative political forces. Such aid, however, was not sufficient to prevent the election of Allende as president of Chile in 1970.

Nixon decided to follow Kissinger's urgings, and thus enhance the clandestine effort to overthrow Allende. In this way, through the CIA, some million dollars were given to Chilean opposition. But the paradox of the way U.S. intelligence acted was that CIA's analysts elaborated more and more optimistic estimates about the political and organizational capacity of groups hostile to Allende, without knowing that they were largely due to secret fundings and aids provided by operative arm of agency itself[87].

The White House had considered two possible courses of action of covert operations in Chile, that would not exclude each other. The first track (track I) foresaw the destabilization of the Chilean economy and the intensification of propaganda against the Allende government. The second (track II), instead, contemplated the extreme outcome of the military coup as well. Actually, this second hypothesis was the one that took place[88].

In September 1973, a military coup put an end to Allende's socialist experiment and brought to power General Augusto Pinochet, who established a strong military dictatorship.

Despite the recent opening of new stores and the disclosure of documents that were previously inaccessible, the degree of involvement of the United States and the CIA in the coup

---

[87] "Fubelt was a secret Central Intelligence Agency program to block the election of Salvator Allende as president of Chile in 1970. In the run-up to the election, the CIA employed propaganda, disinformation, and scare tactics in its attempt to persuade Chileans not to vote for the Social Democrats and Allende [...]. Coup planning included contacting like-minded Chilean military officers, providing them weapons, conducting propaganda to create the political conditions for a coup, and taking actions to destabilize Chile's economy" (Turner M.A., Historical Dictionary of United States Intelligence, cit., p. 77).

[88] See Turner M.A., Historical Dictionary of United States Intelligence, cit., p. 54.

of 1973 is still difficult to ascertain. It is clear, however, that the hostility of the Nixon administration against Allende contributed significantly to determine this outcome.

2.7. **In Nicaragua, the Iran-Contra affair**

The presidential elections of 1980 were largely won by Ronald Reagan. Its success was mostly due to the promise of enhancing the role and credibility of the United States in the world, putting an end to the crisis caused by the uncertainty of Carter and the ruthlessness of Nixon and Kissinger. Reagan's program was appealing to a public opinion focused on increasingly conservative positions[89]. The new president proposed a return to the traditional categories of the Cold War: counteract the action of communism wherever it had occurred and vouch for the clear superiority of the Member against their Soviet enemy.

The new policy envisaged a prominent role for the CIA. During the election campaign, Reagan expressed, on several occasions, his intention to release the CIA from the constraints

---

[89]   "The desire for such a period [Cold War] invites such a political stance, celebrating the past and assuring the future while ignoring the present. Such Presidential representation, then, is appropriate for a time of interludic normalcy; it would be appropriate for a period of either catastrophe or movement, which call for instrumental action" (Combs J.E., The Reagan Range: The Nostalgic Myth in American Politics, Bowling State University Press, 1993, p. 20).

imposed by President Carter on its work. The message was appreciated by an electorate increasingly less receptive to criticism of the CIA[90].

As soon as he took office, Reagan appointed a DCI in his trust, relieving Turner from his office and replacing him with the coordinator of his campaign, William Casey. The choice of Casey was purely political, even if the new director had a decent competence in the field, having been part of the both OSS and commissions to evaluate the performance of the CIA, and other intelligence services of the federal government.

As proof of his intention to give the CIA a new central executive, Reagan decided that DCI became part of the presidential cabinet, thus acquiring a formal equality of status with the Secretary of State and of Defense[91]. This decision was the subject of much criticism because it actually attributed a political role to the position of director of community intelligence services.

---

[90] "Reagan had been willing to excuse CIA abuses when he was a member of the Rockfeller Commission that Gerald Ford established in 1975 to investigate the CIA's family jewels [...]. During the interregnum between his election and inauguration Reagan assembled a transition team to recommend measures to enhance the CIA's capability across the board" (Theoharis A.G., The Central Intelligence Agency: Security Under Scrutiny, cit., p. 57).

[91] "In the president-elect's judgement, improving the CIA required a DCI who appreciated that the United States was in danger and was willing to take risks to secure the national interest. It needed William Casey" (Theoharis A.G., The Central Intelligence Agency: Security Under Scrutiny, cit., p. 57).

As had happened in the past, the new administration started the revival of the operational component of the CIA. By adopting the so-called "Reagan Doctrine", the president argued the need to support the anti-communist forces in the Third World. Through illegal channels, the United States returned to finance and arm the anti-government forces in Angola, the mujaihiddin engaged in the Afghan war against the Soviet army and the forces hostile to the philo-vietnamese Cambodian government[92].

As for domestic policy, the decision to strengthen the strategic arsenal and to verify the possibility of creating a missile defense system capable of protecting the American territory (this policy of Reagan passed under the name of *Star Wars*), was based on the premise that the Soviet Union was an aggressive power, given the large investments that the army was doing in those years[93].

---

[92]   "The Reagan Doctrine also shed some light on the place of the Third World in U.S. foreign policy. It is clear from the logic of the initiative that the primary concern with the targets of the strategy stemmed from connections to issues and events outside the Third World itself. That is, the significance of the Third World to the Reagan Doctrine was essentially as an arena in which to confront the Soviet Union (Scott J.M., Deciding to Intervene: The Reagan Doctrine and American Foreign Policy, Duke University Press, 1996, p. 225).

[93]   Gromm W., Ronald Reagan: Our 40th President, Washington, Regnery Publishing, 2011, p. 124.

Like many of his predecessors, Reagan decided not to pay attention to the analysis of the CIA who disagreed with the conclusions reached. In this difficult situation Reagan decided to use the mean of promotion to replace the director of the CIA, Robert Gates, with John McMahon, previously objected due to the question of the Afghan rebels.

The lack of confidence in the estimates of the CIA had the effect of delaying the response to Reagan's proposals for opening of the new Soviet leader Mikhail Gorbachev, and showed how the promises of the American president to strengthen the CIA were limited to the areas that were most useful[94].

The most well-known and controversial covert operations of the Reagan presidency were those promoted in Central America, particularly in Nicaragua. Here, the Sandinista revolution overthrew the pro-US dictatorship of Anastasio Somoza.

---

[94]   In December 1981, Reagan issued an executive order that eliminated many of the restrictions posed by Carter to covert operations within the United States, even if with the ban of implementing projects of assassination. The CIA operatives were then used to make clandestine programs, ranging from financing the Polish trade union Solidarnosc to the arming and training of the Afghan resistance forces (Theoharis A.G., The Central Intelligence Agency: Security Under Scrutiny, cit., pp. 57-60).

At first, the Reagan administration showed its will to stop the aid provided by the socialist government of Nicaragua to the revolutionary groups in El Salvador. But soon it became clear that the real goal was to overthrow the Sandinista government, through the provision of economic and militarily aid to the Contras insurgency forces[95].

The liberal use of covert operations was also facilitated by the support of the Congress. The new President of the Commission of the Senate intelligence was Barry Goldwater, a member of the Republican right wing. Convinced that the CIA was still liberal and democratic, Goldwater challenged the estimates of analysts from the CIA and argued the need for covert operations[96].

At first, the Congress proved reluctant to intervene in Nicaragua, so much so that the decision to place mines in major ports of Nicaragua (implemented by the CIA) was severely censured by Parliament and costed the United States the complaint of International Tribunal in The Hague. This situation led the Congress to strengthen its control on covert operations[97].

---

[95]   Hayward S.F., The Age of Reagan: The Conservative Counterrevolution: 1980-1989, New York, Crown Publishing Group, 2009, p. 354.

[96]   Lees J.D., Turner M., Reagan's First Four Years: A New Beginning?, Manchester University Press, 1988, p. 218.

[97]   Craven D., Winkenweder B., Dialectical Conversions: Donald Kuspit's Art Criticism, Liverpool University Press, 2011, pp. 211-212.

Since the Parliament had blocked any form of support to the contras, Reagan decided to take other roads. The weapons kept coming to the anti—Sandinista rebels either through private help or through the Israeli government, a traditional ally of the United States. The management of operations in Nicaragua was entrusted to Oliver North, one of Reagan's councilors of the National Security Council[98].

In the same month the United States, violating an embargo which they themselves wanted, had started to sell weapons to the Iranian regime, engaged in a bloody war with Iraq. Through this sale, managed by Israel, the U.S. government proposed a twofold objective: to improve relations with Teheran, while helping the more moderate factions of the Iranian regime, and ensure that Iran would strive to ensure to release U.S. citizens kidnapped by pro-Iranian Hezbollah in Lebanon. To these two objectives, North thought of adding a third: using the profits from the sales of weapons to fund the Contras. Once discovered, this operation (called Iran-contra) sparked bitter controversy in the United States, forcing Reagan to open an investigation.

---

98   See Trahair R.C.S., Encyclopedia of Cold War Espionage, Spies, and Secret Operations, cit., p. 120.

The direct involvement of the President was never proved, but the investigation showed the ruthlessness with which the operation was led and the negligence of the political leadership of the country[99].

---

[99] On the Iran-Contra affair: see McQueen B., An Introduction to Middle East Politics, London, Sage, 2013, pp. 113-115.

CHAPTER 3

NEW AND OLD ENEMIES

3.0. **Introduction**

The Iran-contra affair sharpened the differences between the CIA, the Presidency and Congress that lasted for all of the Eighties and Nineties. The latter, moreover, overthrew the line adopted in the early Eighties and tried to bring under its control the activities of the Central Intelligence Organization, subjecting it to new constraints and restrictions.

A few months after the end of the second term of the Reagan administration, the Senate passed a new law that gave greater powers of supervision to the two committees on intelligence, giving the President (and no longer DCI) the responsibility of informing the Congress on the activities of CIA.

The U.S. elections of 1988 were won by George Bush. For the first time in the history of the United States, a former director of the CIA became president. The result was that the Congress passed a law that immediately established the figure of the Inspector General of the CIA, with the task of monitoring that the activities of the Agency met the requirements set by Congress. The agency had also to inform the Chair through periodic reports. As a result, in the years 1989-1991 Bush had to intervene several times with the presidential veto in order to block laws that intended to introduce further restrictions on the freedom of the CIA[100].

In those years the CIA was given the blame for many of President Bush's indecisions in the presence of the collapse of the communist regimes in the USSR and Eastern Europe. The CIA was also accused of failing to provide functional estimates to predict the Iraqi invasion of Kuwait in August 1990.

From there, it began a period of decline of the CIA that, despite the efforts of the Reagan administration, was unable

---

[100]   Goldsmith J., The Terror Presidency: Law and Judgment Inside the Bush Administration, New York, Norton & Co., 2009, p. 91.

to regain the position he held in the years in which Allen Dulles was president[101].

The excesses of covert operations and the efforts to escape any institutional constraints were obviously dictated by a contingent and temporary situation, and their consequences fell on the successors of Dulles.

Reagan's attempt was based on the belief that a revival of the agency could be helped by covert operations unscrupulously managed and against the standards imposed by Congress, but this revival was unable to be convincing because of its excesses and violations against Gorbachev's openings.

As had already happened in the Sixties and Seventies, the difficulties of the CIA at the end of the last century had to be attributed to the indiscriminate use of covert operations, as shown by the situations described below.

---

[101]   "In the 1990s, the agency again and again was caught by surprise with the discovery of some new secret about Iraq's weapons of mass destruction that had been deliberately concealed by Saddam's regime. In short, the CIA had consistently underestimated the threat posed by the Iraqi regime while overestimating the difficulties of defeating that regime in battle. These failures led Washington policymakers generally to doubt CIA estimates regarding Iraq and to err in the opposite direction" (Maranto R., Lansford T., Johnson J., Judging Bush, Stanford University Press, 2009, p. 33)

3.1. **September 11, 2011: the birth of a new threat**

If the attack on the Twin Towers left the public in the greatest dismay, it was not supposed to be the same for the American intelligence services (CIA and FBI) that for long had needed to be aware of some fact of great importance: the free movement in the United States of some of the fiercest Islamic terrorists, and some relevant news about the hijackers[102].

It is hard to find an explanation for these facts; it can be inferred that, despite the activities of intelligence agencies, the U.S. government has knowingly and repeatedly allowed the known terrorists to enter and circulate freely in the country. In particular, according to the Reuters news agency, a few months before the September 11 attacks, the CIA knew that two of the hijackers, who were linked to the organization al-Qaeda, were located in the United States and knew about other terrorists who lived undisturbed in the State. This

---

[102]   Three weeks before the attacks, the CIA and the FBI had learned that two hijackers, Nawaf Alhazmi and Khalid Almihdhar, were in the United States. Their names were explicitly mentioned among the suspected unwanted terrorists in the United States soil, given the strong links with subversive activities, but still, it was not denied entry into the country to these two people nor were arrested later. The same thing can be said in reference to Mohamed Atta, who, although suspected of terrorism, had been authorized to enter the United States to enroll in a flight school in Florida. During his stay in the United States, he was stopped by the police several times, but was never arrested or expelled from the country (see Atkins E., The 9/11 Encyclopedia: Second Edition, Santa Barbara, ABC-Clio, 2011, pp. 684-685)

information was never forwarded to the FBI, that could have tracked down these men, nor to the Immigration and Naturalization Service, which could have expelled them from the country. Indeed, a year and nine months after the CIA had identified them as terrorists, Alhazmi and Almihdhar lived quietly in the United States, using their real names, preserving their driver's license, opening bank accounts and attending training courses.

This anomalous behavior by the CIA produced embarrassing questions, and even today this interruption of the normal flow of information, crucial to the life of the United States and to the international balance of power, it is still inexplicable. It is even more strange that the CIA had already officially established not to take any action against these terrorists[103].

Informed late, FBI acted as the CIA, by failing to transmit the information to the airlines, as it should be done in an

---

[103]   "The terrorist attacks on 11 September 2001 killed many innocent people, traumatized the country, pushed the U.S. government into a new and uncharted nation security direction, and sparked a nation debate over whether the attacks represented an intelligence failure. The debate probably will continue for quite a long time and may not be resolved to anyone's satisfaction. Like many intelligence failure before it, 9/11 will go down in history as an event for which the United States should have been prepared but was not. The important question is whether America's intelligence agencies had anything to do with that unpreparedness" (Turner M.A., Why Secret Intelligence Fails, cit., p. 1).

emergency or in the event of a criminal investigation, however, significant.

When asked several times on the tragic events of 2001 and its prior events, the CIA gave contradictory answers: at first denied having acquired interesting information on the protagonists of the attacks on Towers and the Pentagon, but then slowly admitted of being aware of the presence of such characters in the United States.

3.2. The war in Iraq

After the First Gulf War in 1991, Saddam Hussein, although defeated, remained in power. The embargo imposed by the UN caused extremely onerous consequences for the population (thousands of victims, especially children, and the sick were without medication), but it is bypassed, and some "forbidden" goods arrived in Iraq with the complicity of some Western companies. Saddam repeatedly thwarted controls about to disarmament, triggering a long series of diplomatic incidents. This led to a standoff resolved in November 1998 by President Clinton (in office 1993-2000) that the mini-Anglo-American offensive campaign called Desert Fox seemed to end[104].

The settlement of Republican George W. Bush on January 20th, 2001 introduced a foreign policy that aimed at protecting U.S. interests in the world and an adequate expansion to the potential and the needs of the country. Bush was a few months in office when the attack on the Twin Towers on September 11 shocked the world.

The responsible of these attack were likely to be linked to the terroristic group Al Qaeda, led by Saudi Osama Bin Laden, following the investigation on the Islamic terrorism; however, the U.S. administration considered Iraq, militarily defeated several times in the past by USA as an accomplice in the attack[105]. The option of a "preemptive" war as the only way to permanently disarm Iraq, caused a deep rift between the Western Allies and a crisis in the UN for the first time since the end of World War II. France, Russia and China, permanent members of the Security Council, threatened the

---

104   Hendrickson R.C., The Clinton Wars: The Constitution, Congress, and War Powers, Vanderbilt University Press, 2002, pp. 154-156.

105   "The rise of al-Qaeda represents a major shift in North-South relations for three reasons. Osama bin Laden and his followers were prepared not only to target attacks on US assets, but to do so in a context that would bring the greater results in terms of shock. And their choice of terrorist methods was unusual in the extent to which they were prepared to treat civilian lives as unimportant and some of those civilians were Muslims. What shocked people [...] was the brutality and destruction as a means to the end of scoring a propaganda victory" (Calvert P., Calvert S., Politics and Society in the Developing World, Harlow, Pearson, 2007, p. 250).

use of the veto to thwart American decisions with the consent of Germany and Belgium. The U.S. has enlisted the support of Britain, another member of the Security Council, and now also a military ally. Italy, Spain (which would later withdraw its contingent), Denmark, Portugal, the Netherlands and other European countries that aspired to join the European Union, were in favor of military intervention[106].

The war began on 20 March 2003 and in three weeks the United States caused the fall of the regime by giving evidence of the overwhelming superiority of the latest Western military technology against an opponent still at the same levels of the first Gulf War of 1991. On May 1, President Bush declared the war officially over.

The U.S. government was aiming at a quick normalization of the country, so much so that the Pentagon believed that a contingent of 50,000 soldiers would be enough to ensure safety. In fact, at the end of December 2004, the troops in Iraq were more than 150,000. The weapons of mass destruction owned by Iraq, according to a statement by the U.S. and Britain, have never been found as well as the ties

---

[106]   See Halliday F., Two hours that shook the world: September 11, 2001 : causes and consequences, London, Saqi, 2002.

between Saddam's Iraq and international terrorism were never proved[107].

Iraq has been freed from dictatorship but, to date has not yet been pacified, still devastated by uncontrollable acts of terrorism, popular hostility against the occupying forces and politically instability, even after the January 2005 elections, because of political and religious disagreements among Sunnis, Shiites and Kurds.

During these events, the CIA's role is primarily linked to the estimates relating to the equipment of Iraq, then transmitted to the U.S. government. In the confusion of the war, in fact, one of the main risks was that weapons or nuclear materials were going to get lost, with the possibility of serious consequences for the health of humanity. But the Pentagon did not seem to have seriously considered that possibility, since it did not deployed enough troops to control the ninety sites that were thought to contain dangerous weapons[108].

The most logical possibility was that the data of the secret service (CIA in particular) on Iraq's weapons programs were

---

[107]   Berinsky A.J., In Time of War: Understanding American Public Opinion from World War II to Iraq, The University of Chicago Press, 2009, pp. 76-80.

[108]   "In the aftermath of the September 11, 2001, terrorist attacks followed by the U.S. invasion of Afghanistan and the U.S. invasion of Iraq, two publications represented the council's efforts to provide U.S. policy makers with an assessment of how the world would evolve and to identify opportunities and negative developments that might require policy actions" (Mockaitis T.R., The Iraq War Encyclopedia, Santa Barbara, ABC-Clio, 2013, p. 296).

not as decisive as the President and other administration officials claimed. It appears that the projections reported by Bush in his State of the Union speech in 2003 were based on controversial evidence[109].

Evidently, the president and his advisors, and maybe even some intelligence officials, had falsified the threat posed by Iraq. A panel inside the CIA, while confirming the judgment of the intelligence analysts regarding the programs of Iraq before the war, concluded that there was no convincing evidence to testify the existence of nuclear weapons in Iraq after the departure of U.S. inspectors in 1998.

---

[109]   CIA analysts at the Department of Energy and the State Department came to the conclusion that the aluminium tubes cited by the President, as evidence of the new program for uranium enrichment, would have probably been used to produce conventional artillery systems. Even allegations that Baghdad would have tried to buy uranium from Niger had proved unfounded long before, also because part of the evidence was built on forged documents (Theoharis A.G., The Central Intelligence Agency: Security Under Scrutiny, cit., p. 75).

3.3. The Guantanamo scandal

Guantanamo has continued and continues to represent a serious problem for the U.S. administration. The attention of the U.S. prison on Cuban soil was awakened especially after the scandal started by the media, which has been an open exposé against the inhumane treatment by the United States to prisoners suspected of terrorism[110].

The case concerned, in particular, the investigative methods used for getting information from detainees. These methods were introduced by former Secretary of Defense Rumsfeld, who had published, modified and re-released a list of new techniques of interrogation by military personnel[111].

And it is well known that between 2002 and 2004 a large number of detainees at Guantanamo Bay has suffered all kinds of abuse, came to light thanks to a report by the International Committee of the Red Cross.

More leaks about the status of prisoners emerged from the FBI memoranda, obtained from non-governmental organizations that have appealed to the U.S. Freedom of

---

[110]   See Borelli S., The treatment of Terrorist Suspects Captured Abroad: Human Rights and Humanitarian Law, in Bianchi A. (ed.), Enforcing International Law Norms Against Terrorism, Oxford, Hart Publishing, 2004, p. 39-61.

[111]   For an overall review on this topic see Greenberg KJ, JL Drater (eds), The Torture Papers: the road to Abu Ghaib, Cambridge University Press, 2005.

Information Act, of two books on the subject[112], and by the statement of a chaplain who spoke about his experience in prison[113]. Finally, the same prisoners, once released, have denounced the abuses suffered, and the reportage of journalists who were able to visit the place provided further details.

In this regard it should be noted that in the summer of 2003, the United States, which had invaded Iraq, imprisoned in Guantanamo a large number of prisoners suspected of being affiliated with terrorist organizations, and to meet the emergencies and violent riots against their presence in Iraq, have begun to apply the same treatment to Iraqi prisoners already in Guantanamo.

Most of the interrogations of these prisoners have been conducted in a manner disrespectful of human dignity, and for that reason they represented a serious violation of international law and the International Convention Against Torture, which forbids both the degrading treatment and any sort of physical violence during the interrogations[114].

---

[112] See Saar E., Novak V., Inside the Wire. A Military Intelligence Soldier's Eyewitness Account of Life at Guantanamo Bay, New York, Penguin, 2005.
[113] See Yee J., For God and Country: Faith and Patriotism Under Fire, New York, Public Affairs Books, 2005.
[114] Amnesty International, United States, Human Dignity Denied: Torture and Accountability in the "War on Terror", Human Rights Watch, 2004.

In a 2009 speech, President Obama has raised the solicitations of public opinion to close the prison by reiterating that this would not reinforced, but indeed weaken, the safety of and within the United States[115].

In the war against terrorism, the U.S. government has used precise survey instruments. At the beginning of the last century has been established, for example, the National Counterrorism Center, with the task of collecting, from various U.S. agencies, information on terrorists. At this point even the FBI and the CIA have enhanced their capacity to collect information and investigations, while the government has reduced the limits on the mutual exchange of information[116].

On the other hand, however, the recent trend of Obama, sought to impose limitations even to the intelligence agencies concerning the specific treatment of terrorists[117]. Also during

---

115   "Instead of building a durable framework for the struggle against al Qaeda that drew upon our deeply held values and traditions, our government was defending positions that undermined the rule of law" (Remarks by the President On National Security, May 21, 2009—http://www.whitehouse.gov - accessed January 2014).

116   "Within the sprawling U.S. Intelligence Community, the National Couterrorism Center (NCTC) was specifically established to bring together all available information on terrorism, analyze the information, and provide warming of potential attacks on the U.S" (Best B.A., National Counter-Terrorism Center (NCTC): Responsibilities and Potential Congressional Concerns, Darby, Diane Publications, 2011, p. 1.

117   In February 2009, for example, was approved a bill introduced by Senator Feinstein that the CIA interrogators demanded to abide to the Army manual, which does not allow harsh interrogation and guarantees the rights also to those detainees considered terrorists (see Newton L., Counterterrorism and Cybersecurity: Total Information Awareness, New York, Springer, 2013, p. 34).

this period, Obama informed the CIA that they would have another president (Panetta).

Although the link between political power and the intelligence agency had historical precedents, Obama's decision was interpreted as a veiled criticism of the Authority.

CONCLUSIONS

Secret intelligence stories made up different images in people's mind. Some consider it as a world of secrets and intrigue that occupies the world of phantasy and animates a series of spy novels, films and sitcoms from which most people get their information about intelligence. Other look at intelligence as a source of evil, a hidden world of secrecy and deception, in the name of which some are authorised to carry out nefarious acts as political assassinations.

On the other hand, intelligence professionals have a different point of view. They consider intelligence as a particular way to get information useful for the political world. To political leaders intelligence indeed may be a political asset or liability, depending on whether intelligence action helps of hinders the fulfilment of political aims.

However perceived, secret intelligence evokes strong passions both in proponents and in opponents. These passions arise mostly because it is the result of controversial aspects of the foreign policy administration and therefore put in touch different points of views and opinions. In any case, the secret intelligence should be intended as illuminating and supporting the foreign policy objectives of whichever foreign administration of a country while it is one of actors at international level.

The consequence of a high number of perspectives concerning the secret intelligence is that its main mission, that is to help the governmental activity, may be missed in favour of an adventure approach.

The studies reviewed here, which are only a part of the extensive literature on the subject of secret intelligence, take into account different angles of the topic, sometimes insisting on the relationship between the CIA and the U.S. government, other times taking an internationalist perspective.

There is no doubt that the activities of the CIA sparked several scandals at the international level and that the consequences that have occurred at times have had a strong impact on public opinion.

There is therefore a strong disconnect between the image of the secret intelligence that comes from the fiction and the real one and yet still many dark areas on its work.

REFERENCES

Texts

Amnesty International, *United States, Human Dignity Denied: Torture and Accountability in the "War on Terror"*, Human Rights Watch, 2004.

Atkins E., *The 9/11 Encyclopedia: Second Edition*, Santa Barbara, ABC-Clio, 2011.

Bandy J., Roberts P., *Hall, Sir William Reginald*, in Tucker S., ed., *World War: A Student Encyclopedia*, Santa Barbara, ABC-Clio, 2006, pp. 857-858.

Barrett D.M., *The Cia And Congress: The Untold Story From Truman To Kennedy*. Lawrence, University Press of Kansas, 2005.

Barrett K., *Truth Jihad: My Epic Struggle against the 9/11 Big Lie*, Joshua Tree, Progressive Press, 2007.

Bentley D.A., *Bruce-Lovett Report*, in Hastedt G.P. ed., *Spies, Wiretaps, and Secret Operations*, Santa Barbara, ABC-Clio, 2011.

Berinsky A.J., *In Time of War: Understanding American Public Opinion from World War II to Iraq*, The University of Chicago Press, 2009.

Best B.A., *National Counter-Terrorism Center (NCTC): Responsibilities and Potential Congressional Concerns*, Darby, Diane Publications, 2011, p. 1.

Blight J.G., Velch D.A., *Intelligence and the Cuban Missile Crisis*, Abingdom, Routledge, 2013.

Blum W., *Killing Hope: Military and CIA interventions Since World War II*, London Zed Books, 2003.

Borelli S., *The treatment of Terrorist Suspects Captured Abroad: Human Rights and Humanitarian Law*, in Bianchi A. (ed.), *Enforcing International Law Norms Against Terrorism*, Oxford, Hart Publishing, 2004, p. 39-61.

Bratich J.Z., *Spies like us*, in Packer J., ed., *Secret Agents: Popular Icons Beyond James Bond*, New York, Peter Lang Publishing, 2009, 132-144.

Brogi A., *A question of Self-Esteem: The United States and the Cold War Choices in France and Italy, 1944-1958*, Westport, Praeger Publisher, 2002.

Brugioni D.A., *Eyes in the Sky: Eisenhower, the CIA, and Cold War Aerial Espionage*, Annapolis, Naval Institute Press, 2010.

Bruneau T., *Patriots for Profits: Contractors and the Military in U.S. National Security*, Stanford University Press, 2011, p. 88).

Bury E., *Eisenhower and the Cold War Arm Race*, London, Tauris & Co., 2014.

Calvert P., Calvert S., *Politics and Society in the Developing World*, Harlow, Pearson, 2007.

Chester E.T., *Covert Network: Progressive, the International Rescue Committee, and the CIA*, Sharpe, New York, 1995.

Ciment J., Hill K., *Encyclopedia of Conflict Since World WarII*, Abingdom, Routledge, 1999.

Combs J.E., *The Reagan Range: The Nostalgic Myth in American Politics*, Bowling State University Press, 1993.

Colonna Vilasi A., *The History of MI6*, Authorhouse-Penguin.

Colonna Vilasi A., *The History of Mossad*, Authorhouse-Penguin.

Cordesman A.H., *The Iraq War: Strategy, Tactics, and Military Lessons*, Washington, Center for Strategic and International Studies, 2003.

Corke S.-J., *US Covert Operations and Cold War Strategy: Truman, Secret Warfare and the CIA, 1945-53*, Abingdom, Routledge, 2008.

Craven D., Winkenweder B., *Dialectical Conversions: Donald Kuspit's Art Criticism*, Liverpool University Press, 2011.

Crosswell D.K.R., *Beetle: The Life of General Walter Bedell Smith*, University Press of Kentucky, 2010.

D'Agostino B., *The Middle Class Fights Back: How Progressiv Movements Can Restore Democracy in America*, Santa Barbara, ABC-Clio, 2012.

Darling A.B., *The Central Intelligence Agency. An Instrument of Government to 1950*, The Pennsylvania State University Press, 1990.

Daugherty W., *Executive Secrets: Covert Action and the Presidency*, Lexington, The University Press of Kentucky, 2004.

Davis P.H.J., <u>*Intelligence and Government in Britain and the United States,*</u> Santa Barbara, ABC-Clio, 2012.

Dorril S., MI6: *Inside the Covert World of Her Majesty's Secret Intelligence Service*, New York, Touchstone, 2002.

Dulles A., *The Craft of Intelligence: America's Legendary Spy Master on the Fundamentals of Intelligence Gathering for a Free World*, Washington,Lion Press, 2006.

Duyal D.H., *Historical Dictionary of the Spanish American War*, Westport, Greenwood Press, 1996.

Farber S., *The Origins of the Cuban Revolution Reconsidered*, University of North Carolina Press, 2006.

Farthoff R.L., *Reflections on the Cuban Missile Crisis*, Washington, Brookings Institution Press, 1989.

Finnegan J.P., *The Military Intelligence Story. A Photo Istory*, Washington, U.S. Government Printing Office, 1998.

Garthoff D.F., *Directors of Central Intelligence as Leaders of the U.S. Intelligence Community, 1946-2005*, Washington, Potomac Books, 2007.

Gleijeses P., *Shattered Hope: The Guatemalan Revolution and the United States, 1944-1954*, Princeton University Press, 1991.

Godson R., *Dirty tricks or Trump Card: U.S. Covert Action and Counterintelligence*, New Brunswick, Transaction Publishers, 2001.

Goldman J., *Ethics of Spying: A Reader for the Intelligence Professional*, Plymouth, Scarecrow Press, 2010.

Goldsmith J., *The Terror Presidency: Law and Judgment Inside the Bush Administration*, New York, Norton & Co., 2009, p. 91.

Greenberg KJ, JL Drater (eds), *The Torture Papers: the road to Abu Ghaib*, Cambridge University Press, 2005.

Gromm W., *Ronald Reagan: Our 40th President*, Washington, Regnery Publishing, 2011.

Grose P., *Gentleman Spy: The Life of Allen Dulles*, University of Massachusetts Press, 1996.

Halliday F., *Two hours that shook the world: September 11, 2001 : causes and consequences*, London, Saqi, 2002.

Hansche S., Berti J-. Hare C., *Official (ISC)2 Guide to the CISSP Exam*, Boca Raton, Auerbach Publications, 2004.

Hastedt G.P., *Encyclopedia of American Foreign Policy*, New York, Facts On File, 2004.

Hayward S.F., *The Age of Reagan: The Conservative Counterrevolution: 1980-1989*, New York, Crown Publishing Group, 2009.

Hendrickson R.C., *The Clinton Wars: The Constitution, Congress, and War Powers*, Vanderbilt University Press, 2002.

Hillstrom K., *The Cold War*, Detroit, Omnigraphics, 2006.

Immermann R.H., *The CIA in Guatemala: The Foreign Policy of Intervention*, University of Texas Press, 2010.

Jeffery K., *MI6: The History of the Secret Intelligence* Service 1909-1949, London, Crowd, 2010.

Johnson L.K., *America's Secret Power*, New York, Oxford University Press, 1989.

Johnson L.K., *Strategic Intelligence*, Westport, Preager Security International, 2007, vol. 3, p. 162.

Kaiser D.E., *American Tragedy: Kennedy, Johnson, and the Origins of the Vietnam War*, Harvard University Press, 2000.

Kihss P., *Adm. Roscoe H. Hillenkoetter, First Director of the C.I.A.*, "The New York Times", June 21, 1982.

Kilby K., *My Silent War: the Autobiography of a Spy*, London, Arrow Books, 2003.

Landers J., *The Weekly War: Neswmagazines and Vietnam*, University of Missouri Press, 2004.

Leary W.M., *The Central Intelligence Agency, History and Documents*, University of Alabama Press, 1984.

Lees J.D., Turner M., *Reagan's First Four Years: A New Beginning?*, Manchester University Press, 1988.

Liptak E., *Office of Strategic Services 1942-1945. The World War II. Origin of the CIA*, Oxford, Osprey Publishing, 2013.

Malkasian C., *The Korean War*, New York, The Rosen Publishing Group, 2009.

Manweller M., *Chronology of the U.S. Presidency*, Santa Barbara, ABC-Clio, 2012.

Maranto R., Lansford T., Johnson J., *Judging Bush*, Stanford University Press, 2009.

Marrs J., *Crossfire: The Plot who Killed Kennedy*, New York, Basic Books, 2010.

McQueen B., *An Introduction to Middle East Politics*, London, Sage, 2013.

Miscamble W.D., *George F. Kennan and the Making of American Foreign Policy, 1947-1950*, Princeton University Press, 1992.

Mockaitis T.R., *The Iraq War Encyclopedia*, Santa Barbara, ABC-Clio, 2013, p. 296.

Montague L.L., *General Walter Bedell Smith as Director of Central Intelligence*, October 1950—February 1953, The Pennsylvania University Press, 1992.

National Defence (ed.), *LSA List of CFR*, 32, Washington, U.S. Government Printing Office, part 800 to End, revised as of July 1, 2003.

Newton L., *Counterterrorism and Cybersecurity: Total Information Awareness*, New York, Springer, 2013.

Paddock A.H. jr, *U.S. Army Special Warfare. Its Origins. Psychological and Unconventional Warfare*, 1941-1952, Honolulu, University Press of the Pacific, 2002.

Prados J., *Safe for Democracy: The Secret Wars of the CIA*, Chicago, Ivan R. Dee, 2006.

Raskin M.G., *The Politics of National Security*, New Brunswick, Transaction, 1979.

Saar E., Novak V., *Inside the Wire. A Military Intelligence Soldier's Eyewitness Account of Life at Guantanamo Bay*, New York, Penguin, 2005.

Scott J.M., *Deciding to Intervene: The Reagan Doctrine and American Foreign Policy*, Duke University Press, 1996.

Smith W.T., *Encyclopedia of the Central Intelligence Agency*, New York, Facts On File, 2003.

Spencer C.T., *The European Powers in the First World War: An Encyclopedia*, New York, Routledge, 2013,.

Srode J., *Allen Dulles: Master of Spies*, Washington, Regnery Publishing, 1999.

Stone D., *Holocaust Testimony and the Challenge of the Philosophy of History*, in Fine R., Turner Ch., eds, *Social Theory After the Holocaust*, Liverpool University Press, 2000, pp. 219-234.

Stuart D.T., *Creating the National Security State: A History of the Law that Transformed America*, Princeton University Press, 2008,.

Theoharis A.G., *The Central Intelligence Agency: Security Under Scrutiny*, Westport, Greenwood Press, 2006.

Trahair R.C.S., *Encyclopedia of Cold War Espionage, Spies, and Secret Operations*, Enigma Books, New York, 2013.

Tucker S.C., *The Encyclopedia of the Vietnam War*, Santa Barbara, ABC-Clio, 2011.

Tudda C., *The Truth is Our Weapon: The Rhetorical Diplomacy of Dwight D. Eisenhower and John Foster Dulles*, Louisiana University Press, 2006.

Turner M.A., *Historical Dictionary of United States Intelligence*, Lanham, Scarecrow Press, 2006.

Turner M.A., *Why Secret Intelligence Fails*, Dulles, Potomac Books, 2005.

US Central Intelligence Agency—CIA—*Handbook. Strategic information, activities and regulations*, Washington, International Business Publications, 2013.

Wynn N.A., *The A to Z of the Roosevelt-Truman Era*, Lanham, Rowman & Littlefield Publishing, 2008.

Yee J., *For God and Country: Faith and Patriotism Under Fire*, New York, Public Affairs Books, 2005.

Websites

www.cia.gov.

www.sourcewatch.org http://www.whitehouse.gov

I would like to thank Dr Federico Conforto
and the Italian Book club.